Who was Verlon "Rube" Walker?

"He was the wit of the Cubs and often the heart. He was the man who always said the right thing at the tense moment...the man who dashed into a free-for-all at Wrigley Field last summer for one reason: to shield rival (Pittsburgh Pirates) Manager Danny Murtaugh, who recently had suffered a heart attack."

—*Rick Talley, late award-winning columnist for The Chicago Tribune*

"He is as droll as Will Rogers, and almost every day he comes up with a wisecrack that helps ease the tension of a long season."

—Ernie Banks, *"Mr. Cub," late Chicago Cubs shortstop and Baseball Hall of Famer*

"He was a true gentleman, a kind man."

—Fergie Jenkins, *Chicago Cubs Pitcher and Baseball Hall of Famer*

"He was mild-mannered. All the players respected him. When he spoke, we listened."

—Billy Williams, *Chicago Cubs Outfielder and Baseball Hall of Famer*

From the author:

A girl without a father has no ground, no gravity. She floats through life without that invisible force holding her feet to the earth. Cascading softly through the stratosphere, twisting gracefully, somersaulting with wispy glittering elegance like a star. Ethereal. A little lost star. If you're a father to a daughter **let me be clear....** without you, she is lost in the world. You are her gravity. You give her that section of real estate under her feet. A plot of land to call her own, which can never be revoked. In your eyes she sees her value. A girl can live without it – I have. My life hasn't been sullen and catastrophic. It's just that life is more peaceful when you have ground under your feet and know your worth.

As I reflect upon my journey to know my father, I feel overwhelming gratitude for all the people who have shared my journey and helped propel me forward. I am healed by their stories and blessed by my father's legacy as a kind and memorable man. This book is a detailed account of me finding my ground. It is a roadmap of my worth.

Requests for permission should be addressed to: Ascend Books, LLC, Attn: Rights and Permissions Department, 7221 West 79th Street, Suite 206, Overland Park, KS 66204

10 9 8 7 6 5 4 3 2 1

ISBN: print book 978-0-9989224-0-9
ISBN: e-book 978-0-9989224-1-6
Library of Congress Control Number: 2017941642

Publisher: Bob Snodgrass
Editor: Teresa Bruns Sosinski
Publication Coordinator: Heather Phelan
Sales and Marketing: Lenny Cohen
Dust Jacket and Book Design: Rob Peters
Cover photo by Barney Sterling

All photos courtesy of the author unless otherwise indicated. Every reasonable attempt has been made to determine the ownership of copyright.

The goal of Ascend Books is to publish quality works. With that goal in mind, we are proud to offer this book to our readers. Please notify the publisher of any erroneous credits or omissions, and corrections will be made to subsequent editions/future printings. Please note, however, that the story, experiences, and the words are those of the authors alone.

Printed in The United States of America

www.ascendbooks.com

FINDING
My Father's
VOICE
A Baseball
Love Story

Leigh Ann Walker
with Chuck Carlson
Foreword by Pat Hughes, Chicago Cubs Radio Play-by-Play Broadcaster

Contents

Dedication

I dedicate this book to those with grieving hearts everywhere, especially my mother.

Foreword
by Pat Hughes

*L*eigh Ann Walker swept into my life a few years ago, full of enthusiasm, full of doubt and emotion and, mostly, full of questions for which she was hoping to find answers.

She wanted to know about her father, Verlon Walker, who had spent nearly a decade with the Chicago Cubs, first as part of the eclectic but ultimately doomed College of Coaches in 1961 and then as a valuable right-hand man for that force-of-nature manager Leo Durocher.

Verlon Walker, known to everyone as "Rube," had seen everything in baseball, as a player/manager in the low minors and then ultimately as the Cubs' bullpen coach. He had seen the good and the bad with the Cubs, as most Cubs' fans have as well.

He was in the dugout in 1969 when that black cat ran across Ron Santo's feet and the division-leading Cubs eventually collapsed and lost out to the New York Mets. He was there to see Cubs' immortals like Ferguson Jenkins and Billy Williams and Ernie Banks become the toast of the town. But he was also there for all of those young players over the years, those unknown players who needed some advice, some encouragement and someone to tell them they had that chance to prove they belonged.

Those were the players Rube probably felt closest to because he had been one of them. And from what Leigh Ann told me about her dad, that's the way he wanted it.

Whether a Hall of Famer or a regular guy, everyone said the same thing about Rube Walker: He was one of the truly good people in the game. Blessed with insight, a dry southern wit and a keen understanding of people, Rube made everyone feel like they'd known him forever. It was a rare and wonderful gift.

But Rube was struck down with leukemia in 1971, during spring training prior to the season when he was to claim the job he'd always wanted: pitching coach for the Cubs. Rube died in March of that year at the age of 42, leaving behind his wife Ann and his three-year-old little girl, Leigh Ann.

And now Leigh Ann, grown and with children of her own, had found me and was hoping I could help her recapture the voice of her father, the voice she had never known from a man she barely knew.

As the Cubs' play by play announcer for WGN since 1996, I had a few connections within the organization and did my small part to help move her investigation along. I was rooting for her to find what she was looking for.

And her story resonated around baseball. Her search has been featured in stories on MLB.com, in newspapers and on TV. Her single-mindedness in finding out about her father is worthy of any detective story and I was pleased I could be a small part of it.

I met her in person for the first time in the summer of 2015 when she came to Chicago to watch the Cubs and to visit the Rube Walker Blood Center (named for her father) at Northwestern Memorial Hospital. And I could tell how important this journey was for her.

Leigh Ann has now turned that quest into a book about the long, involved, sometimes painful, journey to discover just who her father was.

She has delved deep inside her to talk about the pain and anguish and longing that has been such a part of her life since her father died. She has found people who remembered him well and have told the stories that have produced an image of the man. She also found a recording of him giving a brief talk in his native Lenoir, North Carolina, putting a voice to the man.

In truth, she has not written this book for Chicago Cubs fans or even baseball fans, though they're more than welcome to join in on the journey. She wrote this for a larger audience of people who have suffered loss in their lives and are still looking for ways to cope with it. It's not an easy subject to write about but one that needed to be done.

In October 2016, when the Cubs ended their 108-year drought and won the World Series, an entire city and, yes, much of the country celebrated, too. And joining in was Leigh Ann Walker, who followed the Cubs from her North Carolina home for every game during that magical season. For her, those Cubs were a chance for her to once again reconnect with her father.

And it's hard to imagine he wasn't watching every inning himself. And smiling.

Introduction

A few days ago, I dreamed of him.

We were sitting in a blue pickup truck drinking coffee. He was wearing a light brown hunting jacket with a dark brown corduroy collar. One hand on the wheel the other holding a Styrofoam cup. Steam rising. He was laughing. It felt real. It was warm like flesh and breath.

I woke up.

I closed my eyes tightly to put myself back in that truck, but it was gone. He was gone. The way dreams just fade away once you realize they are dreams.

Laying there replaying the dream in my mind, it occurred to me that *I* had put flesh and breath there. I've heard that when people master a new language, they begin to dream in that language. That's what I had done. I had gone on a grand adventure to find out everything I could about my father and three years later, I had dreamed of him. Gathering memories, looking deep into pictures, hearing his voice, listening to stories were all a form of mastery. I had essentially brought him to me. He felt real and now I missed him.

My dad's name was Verlon Lee Walker but everyone called

him Rube. He was a coach for the Chicago Cubs from 1961 to 1972. Actually, my father's nickname was "Little Rube" because his big brother was "Rube."

Al "Rube" Walker was three years older than my dad and more well-known in the baseball world. He played 11 seasons in the big leagues as a catcher, from 1948-58, with the Chicago Cubs and the Brooklyn Dodgers, where he was a teammate of one of the game's transformative figures, Jackie Robinson. My uncle completed his career with the Dodgers when the team moved to Los Angeles.

Eventually my dad's nickname of "Little Rube" was shortened to "Rube," making my quest to find out about him a bit more confusing. Two former Major Leaguers named Rube? Really?

Nevertheless, I had a family with an interesting baseball legacy which up until now I had neglected.

When I was three, my father died of leukemia. As a little girl, I never talked about it. I had an unspoken pact with anyone close to me. *I won't talk about it so don't ask any questions.* That was my defense, as if pretending my father didn't exist would dissolve the grief.

It didn't dissolve. Instead the grief held me hostage. It bound me in invisible cords limiting my emotional ability. I didn't allow myself to connect to people because I knew the unthinkable does happen: people you need, die. Don't get too close, it will only hurt when they go. I was a numbed-out master of disguise.

On my 42nd birthday my husband gave me a pink baseball glove with a note saying, "A coach's daughter should have her own glove."

The poignancy of that sentence resonated. My teeth rattled at the truth of it. I was a coach's daughter, but I didn't know what that meant. The grief that I had packed away came rushing to the surface. My throat felt tight. I closed my eyes and tears squeezed from the corners. I held my breath. My father died at 42. I was 3 when he died.

Now I was 42 and my youngest son was 3. It was a mash-up of time and emotion. I pulled my son onto my lap. I can remember what he felt like that morning. The warmth of his little body, the weight of his legs on mine, a gurgle in his tummy, the smell of him, his tapping fingertips wrapped around the fleshy part of my upper arm. My father and I had said good bye to this many years ago. I don't remember what his lap felt like, what he smelled like, or his embrace.

Just another story of loss? Maybe, but it was my story and I was finally ready to own it. Girl loses her father, spends years pretending

I made my pilgrimage to Wrigley Field in Chicago in 2015 to find out more about my father and the legacy he left behind with the Chicago Cubs and the people of Chicago. What I found has offered me a view of my father that I never knew about and, frankly, never really expected. (Photo courtesy Johnny Burbano Photography)

she is fine, realizes she isn't and decides to do something about it. It was that simple. Here's what I decided to do.

I've been asked many times what made me start the quest to get to know my father. I can't really pinpoint one main event. While turning the age my father was when he died and the gift of the glove helped jar me into action, long before that there was a stirring inside me that propelled me forward. I became hungry for him. So hungry, I was willing to face the grief I knew would envelope and, at times, overtake me. It would be worth it, of that I was certain.

Approaching my quest initially as a fact-finding research project I set about gathering everything I had in one place. Dusty boxes that included pictures, letters, cuff links, lighters, a pair of glasses, a deck of cards, a ring, a bat. My father's life reduced to a few boxes under a bed. I sifted through them slowly, taking short sabbaticals from my daily life to be with him.

All the years of ignoring my father meant I had no emotional connection to the boxes of stuff. He was a stranger. I didn't lose him. I never had him. It registered more as a void. It was a gaping hole the size of him that nothing could fill.

Over the next few years I would try to infuse those boxes with his essence by layering flesh on bone hoping to create a man. I wanted a glimpse into his personality, I wanted to hear his voice, I wanted to see the way he walked. I wanted to know his likes and dislikes.

Nothing was insignificant. Tiny details of knowing that most people take for granted, I yearned for. Did he like sunflower seeds? I didn't know that, but I wanted to.

This was a big change for me because, as a child, I didn't always look at those boxes. I couldn't. The boxes were always around and stored on a shelf of the guest bedroom closet. I knew they were there and ignored them because they were just too painful to look at. I was afraid to open the boxes.

The first time I started investigating them was in college. I would look through a few pictures late at night and then put them away exactly as they were. It was a gradual process going to that well of picture memories. I would start to feel sad about what I had missed and pull away from it. I wasn't ready.

In the back of my mind I knew I needed to grieve, but I didn't know how. I had always felt uncomfortably sad as I walked through life in the skin I was given. Something wasn't quite right inside me. I could feel it but couldn't speak it. The fact that I had zero memories of him, no words of wisdom, no advice, no special moments made it easy to avoid. I thought maybe this might be a way to do that but I wasn't sure. And I was afraid. But then I found that inner strength I wasn't sure I had. I think it's like when people have fathers they grow up with and their fathers gave them guidance and bits of wisdom and advice. I didn't have that and I had this gaping abyss, this hole, inside me. I neglected it until I couldn't anymore.

Necessity more than courage launched me forward. I started a blog in 2011 in order to have a footprint on the internet. I decided I would share my photographs and story in hopes that more would come to me. Obviously, people have to know that I'm looking in order to help me. By the way, asking for help is not my forte.

I began by emailing Pat Hughes, the Chicago Cubs play-by-play radio announcer for the past 20 years, in hopes that he could connect me with collectors in Chicago who might have radio or TV archives from the 1960s. Finding a video or audio recording of my father was my primary focus in the beginning.

Much to my surprise Pat responded. He put me in touch with George Castle – an author, baseball historian and Chicago native. George became my guide and writing mentor. His involvement in my journey has been paramount. He shared his baseball knowledge, contacts and experience with me. With his leadership, I began to focus on gathering stories from people who knew my dad.

In November of 2013 Keith Olbermann highlighted my story on his ESPN show. This national attention was a boost to the readership of my blog as well as interest in my quest. I was both excited by and uncomfortable with the attention.

Taking such a personal journey in a public way was a bit overwhelming. Once Olbermann ran the story a shift occurred. People were interested in my journey. I had set out to discover my dad and his voice and in the process discovered myself and my voice. As a result, my entire life changed.

In the chapters to follow, I will try to convey a story of loss, uncertainty, recovery and triumph. Hopefully, it will be more about recovery and triumph but, as I learned, all of it runs together – the good and bad. One does not exist without the other.

I've learned, and am still learning, there is no right way, no best way, no easy way to deal with these kinds of agonizing losses. Everyone's path is unique. I needed to take this journey to heal myself. I had no idea what I was doing or how it would turn out. I just chose to start.

I hope this story inspires anyone else who might be struggling with grief weeks, months, years, or like me, decades later. This quest is my emancipation from grief.

This story is my crucible but it's a universal story of transformation. You don't have to be a servant to the sadness. There is hope.

CHAPTER 1
Simply, Verlon Walker

*E*verything I know about him was either told to me or I read in a book. I have no memories of my own.

Is that unusual? I don't really know. Illness, accidents and war have taken many parents. I wasn't alone in that feeling of emptiness.

Disney begins just about every movie by killing off the mother. Both Cinderella and Snow White's parents died. Bambi's mother is killed right in front of him. One minute she's there, the next minute he is alone in the woods. The harsh Disney lesson: life is fragile. Things happen beyond your control and impact the rest of your life. I learned that firsthand, but was it unusual that my dad felt like a stranger?

The first time I remember feeling the absence of my father was in kindergarten. I attended a half-day school that was held at the Baptist church where my mother is still an active member.

We napped, snacked, colored, put seeds in a Dixie cup to see if they would grow, and played. I was painfully shy and enjoyed the solitary act of swinging when the teacher took us to the playground. A little girl came up to me as I ran to the swing and asked me if my daddy ever pushed me on the swing.

I shook my head no.

She continued to tell me about how her dad pushes her "real high" so she can jump off, but her mother doesn't like it.

"I don't have a dad," I blurted out.

I don't remember her exact words but she said something to the effect of, I had to have a dad because everyone has a dad.

I didn't have a ready answer, so I said nothing.

Years later when I was ready to embark on my quest, my goal was to build a man that would bring me solace. The one I had wished for that day on the playground.

I started with what I knew, layering on what I learned. I wanted to make him real. He had always been a ghost to me; a haunting illusion beyond my comprehension. There was evidence he had existed but to me, he was fictitious. I had never seen him, felt him or heard him.

Growing up, I would have a flash of yearning for my father which would initiate a data gathering phase followed by the complete inability to cope with what I discovered.

One time I researched my own father's height. He was six feet tall. I sourced that information from a baseball book and tucked it inside me for reference. The next day, I marked six feet on my bedroom wall with a pencil and stood beside it. I tried to picture his face up at the mark, but I needed more.

A few weeks later at church, I asked some of the older gentlemen how tall they were. When I found one that was six feet tall, I hugged him. I wanted to see what six feet tall felt like in the flesh. My head reached the center of his chest. I closed my eyes and I rested my ear against the man's heart to hear it beating. I was 14.

That's when I began my search for my value in a man's heart.

My first boyfriend was a baseball player, of course, and a good one, too. I noticed him for the first time one night at

Burger King, the meeting place of kids with transportation in my small town.

He was sitting at one of those earth-toned plastic tables. I walked past his table and sat down with my friends. He had amazing blue eyes that could liquefy glass. I pursued him. I don't remember the details, but within a few weeks, I had a date.

My dad, Verlon "Rube" Walker, died March 24, 1971 at the age of 42. I was 3 years old at the time and his loss has impacted me my entire life. So, I decided to go in search of the man I never really knew and that search has lasted three years and continues. (Photo courtesy of James D. McCarthy)

We fell in love – crazy, engulfing, nothing's-more-important-in-the-world teenage love. I wrapped my life around his. It felt right and filled me up. I was 17.

This baseball player loved me. He made me laugh. He made me feel special and beautiful. My senior year of high school and the summer after graduation were blissful, but we went away to different colleges. I could not handle being apart. I didn't know how to love him and be without him. The lack of him broke me. It registered as a form of abandonment.

Another man I needed was gone.

The truth was, he had not abandoned me. He was a teenager living his life. When he didn't seem destroyed by the distance in the same manner I was, I assumed he was disconnecting from me and would eventually leave. I walled up my heart and let him go.

I concluded I was too sensitive for relationships but I didn't really want to be alone. I was love-challenged. My solution: keep men at a safe emotional distance and don't fall in love with baseball players.

Boyfriend after boyfriend would try to rescue me from myself. I reveled in the attention but treated each one as a passing phase, positive they would eventually leave anyway.

Most of them didn't want to leave, but I made it impossible for them to stay. I purposely wore them out with my antics, creating the self-fulfilling abandonment prophecy. There was a shield around my heart that they couldn't see and would never be able to penetrate. It was also my buffer from pain.

In hindsight, being in a relationship with me was rather confusing. I put forth a damsel in distress persona but when superman swooped in to save me, I refused to let him. Emotional dependence was risky. I just couldn't give someone the power to hurt me. I had a crippling fear of being abandoned.

Searching for male approval through romantic relationships

had proven painful, so I began looking to older gentlemen, father-figure types, to provide the validation I thought I needed.

I had a college professor take an interest in me. He had a big laugh, an eloquent manner and a quick wit. I would visit him weekly to discuss politics, poetry, my future, sports. I built a relationship with him and confided in him about my battle with depression and the struggle to find the right chemical compound to fix me.

One Friday afternoon I stopped by his office before leaving for spring break. I plopped down in the chair beside his desk. He was facing me with his legs crossed. I began complaining about the work load I was forced to endure prior to leaving for break. In the middle of my monologue, he playfully tapped my foot with his and said, "So, when are we going to make love?"

I looked down at his foot. I wanted to pretend those words had not been spoken, but they hung there between us. Before he could say anything else, I stood up and walked out.

I had been so happy just minutes before. My fantasy of fatherly love disintegrated. The ground I was standing on eroded right out from under me. It was jarring. I questioned my actions. Had I done something to make him think we would one day be intimate? I went over my actions in my head. It is possible that I flirted with him. I blamed myself for inviting his comment. I never saw him again. I was 19.

I wish I could tell you I learned from that interaction with my college professor, but the search for fatherly approval was intoxicating to me.

My stepfather had told me, "Little girls are to be seen and not heard." When a man fostered my intellectual development ignoring the way I looked, I could not resist his attention. I craved it and would end up repeating this pattern several more times until my self-esteem deteriorated and I trusted no man.

I wasn't always searching for my father. Sometimes a piece

of him would come to me.

My dad was well-known and well-liked in his hometown. Occasionally, I would run into people who would recognize me as his daughter. They would feel compelled to talk to me about him as the sight of me made them remember him.

One evening, I was standing in the grocery check-out line buying wine when a man I did not know came up and said, "Aren't you Verlon Walker's daughter?"

"I am! Did you know him?" I responded proudly.

"Everybody knew him. Gosh, you look just like your mama!"

"I get that a lot," I said smiling.

"Let me tell you this," he said, leaning in close. "Years ago I was fishin' over on Lake James one afternoon during the week and ran out of gas. There wasn't a soul out on the lake. Hell, I was supposed to be at work. I knew I had to get home soon or my wife would pitch a fit."

He paused. I was hanging on every word waiting for my dad to appear in the story.

"Here comes your daddy motoring by in his boat. He gave me a beer and towed me back to shore. When we got to the dock, Verlon said, 'Next time I see your wife, I'm gonna tell her what a hard worker you are.' "

The man was enjoying replaying that day in his head.

"He had that dry sense of humor, you know," he added laughing.

I laughed, too, even though I had no idea about my father's sense of humor.

"Were you his friend?" I asked.

"Oh, yeah, I knew him and his brothers," he said. "Between you and me, Verlon was my favorite. He was one of a kind."

Then he pointed at me and asked, "How old were you when he died?"

"I was three," I said in a matter-of-fact-tone.

His smile left. "That's just too bad. Do you remember him?"

"No, not really."

I added the *not really* to soften it for me and him.

There was a pause.

"Thank you for telling me that story." I looked at the man and smiled.

He smiled back at me, "You have a good evenin'," he said and walked away.

A story from a stranger who seemed to know more about my father than I did.

I walked to my car, got in, opened the bottle of wine and drank that story down, word for word, sip for sip. The warmth burned off the emotion. I enjoyed hearing the story but I had nothing to hang it on so I made it go away.

That's when I began to seek comfort in alcohol.

I didn't want to feel the uncomfortable sadness, and alcohol made me feel better. That's me simplifying the complex emotional pain that accompanies grief. Alcohol was my coping mechanism.

I will never forget the first time I put it in my body. The warmth of it as it slid down my throat, creating a glow that radiated out from my chest through my entire body. I felt relaxed. My mind went calm. It altered me in a way that I liked. I would chase that feeling for seven years after the initial introduction.

I quickly hit bottom with alcohol. It just quit working. I couldn't pour enough in me to achieve the anesthetizing effect I desired. The alcohol didn't make me feel the warm glow anymore. It didn't make me feel numb anymore. It was actually making me feel worse. Everything I drank down was coming out sideways in the form of depression.

At 23, I put on some really dark sunglasses and walked into a rehab center. I have lived a sober life ever since, but from the age of 23 to 42 had avoided the root cause of my problem which was the loss of my father.

Avoiding the grief all these years had caused me to act, react and live in dysfunctional ways. It had finally caught me and wrecked me. Decades after the loss of my father, I had to make myself whole again.

Let's start at the beginning. Who was this man and why had the lack of him crushed me?

Verlon Walker's baseball career was a long meandering path through the Chicago Cubs minor league system. He never played a single game in the majors.

In Rick Talley's book, *The Cubs of 1969*, he refers to my dad as the "wit and the heart" of the 1969 Cubs.

Talley recounts my dad's self-deprecating story about beating out Rocky Marciano in a minor-league tryout in 1947. Yes, that Rocky Marciano, who was considered by many boxing experts as one of the greatest heavyweight champions in history.

Apparently, Marciano's first love was baseball and he traveled to eastern North Carolina to try out for the position of catcher on a Cubs' farm team. After three weeks he was cut, losing out to another promising catcher: Verlon Walker, my dad.

Marciano turned to professional boxing in 1948 and four years later, he'd claim the world heavyweight title – a title he would hold until 1956. He retired with a 49-0 record, including 43 knockouts.

In the book Talley quotes my dad, "When Rocky Marciano found out he was a worse catcher than me he got so mad he started beating up people."

It was this self-deprecating sense of humor and kind demeanor that endeared my dad to everyone he met. These were personality traits cultivated in a small town at the base of the Blue Ridge Mountains.

My dad was the unofficial ambassador for Lenoir, North Carolina. When his players would tease him about being from such a small town, he would use his wit to fire back with comments about the "greatness" of Lenoir. There was a *Lenoir News Topic* newspaper article published in 1969 referring to my dad as Lenoir's "Ambassador of Good Will."

Ernie Banks, the Chicago Cubs' Hall of Famer, once asked my dad why the mayor of Lenoir wasn't attending some official conference in Washington, D.C. My dad responded by saying, "He is way too busy to be bothered by such dealings. There are important things going on in Lenoir."

If there is anything like a typical small town, Lenoir was it. The main road into the city is flanked by a golf course on both sides. Maple and hickory trees border rolling hills of grass.

Hibriten Mountain rises up right in the middle to watch over the salt-of-the-earth residents. Lights laid out in the shape of a cross on the radio tower at the top of Hibriten Mountain mark the holy days leading up to Easter. At Christmas, the pattern changes from a cross to a star. These lights can be seen for miles in all directions. It's a tradition started in 1954 that still exists today. A symbol of the far-reaching Christian values in the area. I look forward to seeing the star or the cross each season when I visit.

A charming downtown center with a courthouse, a bank, a movie theater, a hardware store and several locally owned shops anchor the town. Not much has changed since the days my dad grew up there. A mall was built in the 1980's and sucked the life out of the town center. Then Walmart blew in and rendered the mall a ghost town. Currently, there is a revitalization of the downtown.

"Hog Waller" used to be a block behind the center of town. It was a large open-air market where anyone could trade or sell produce, livestock, moonshine or flowers. Really, you could sell just about anything. Street musicians and preachers would converge upon the area to spread their own message. The legendary bluegrass musician, Doc Watson, started his career in Hog Waller.

It was a meeting place of sorts, bringing everyone to town on Saturday. The Walker family lived close by. I can imagine my dad working his way through the place, talking to each vendor. The Hog Waller street market no longer exists, but a grand stage has been built where local musicians play and artists gather.

Lenoir was a factory town with a population of about 7,800 in 1950. Factories churned out hand-crafted furniture that would be shipped all over the country. Several furniture companies headquartered in Lenoir dominated the industry which fueled the economy of the town. This lasted until the 1990's when the furniture companies restructured their businesses, sending much of the furniture-manufacturing out of the United States.

This shift in the industry halted the economic growth of Lenoir. Still quaint, still beautiful, still full of God-loving, salt-of-the-earth people, but economically, the good jobs became scarce and Lenoir became like so many other small towns that had seen better days.

The Walkers labored in the furniture factories and textile mills, then came home to work in their garden. They lived in poverty. Life was sometimes a struggle. On Sundays, they rested, worshipped the Lord, and played baseball.

God, Family, Hard Work and Baseball was the Walker creed.

My dad learned to play baseball with his brothers, Al and Leslie. Their father would bring home yarn from the textile mill and wrap it around golf balls to make a baseball.

The Walker boys spent their youth playing baseball, knocking those home-made balls through the air. Crisscrossing the town on foot, they would pick up anyone interested in playing ball and gather in a field large enough to handle the hits.

They would carve out a baseball diamond using an old cereal box as home plate. Everything was a fair ball until the ball went down the sewer grate or broke the neighbor's basement window. Baseball was America's game. My dad and my uncles were bewitched by it. Before long, the Walker boys were known around town for their baseball skills.

These carefree days of baseball and small-town life certainly made a lasting impression on my dad. He carried a little piece of Lenoir in his heart wherever he went.

Older brother, Albert, who everyone knew as "Rube," would become the most successful baseball player of the three. He played for the Brooklyn Dodgers and coached the New York Mets, winning a World Series with both teams.

Rube was an incredible athlete. Besides being a baseball star, he was also quarterback of the high school championship football team and a pretty decent golfer. He was the typical older brother: disciplined, respectful and serious.

The youngest brother, Leslie, never left Lenoir. He spent his life nurturing baseball at a grassroots level. A respected umpire and Little League coach, Uncle Les was my link to my father. He would take me for rides in his truck, stopping to buy me candy and soda which my mom didn't want me to have. Driving down country roads listening to "Ring of Fire" by Johnny Cash, he told me things my dad would want me to hear.

"You were all he ever wanted, Leigh," Uncle Les said, glancing at me then back at the road.

I smiled. I didn't know what to say.

"He loved baseball but he loved you and your mama more," he said.

When I heard that, I turned my face away from him, looked out the window and cried.

He would return me to my grandmother's house, sugared up and sad. She would say, "Les, she's sensitive, you know."

Uncle Les would wink at me, saying, "Don't get mad at me, Minnie. She's OK."

Then he'd leave me alone there to sort out my emotions under the weeping willow tree in my grandmother's yard. That's where I went to hide. I would lie in the grass smelling the honeysuckle vines that covered the side of a building my grandmother called the smoke house. I wasn't okay like Uncle Les said I was.

Today, a Johnny Cash song can put me back in that pick-up truck with him and the smell of honeysuckle takes me to that weeping willow tree.

> *Dear Weeping Willow Tree,*
> *I come here to be invisible. To blend right in with you and*
>   *the grass.*
> *Your lean flowy branches tickle the ground shielding me.*
> *A barrier of green showing peeks of me.*
> *If my grandmother looks out the dining room window,*
>   *she might see my white tennis shoes with stars and my*
>   *pigtails.*
> *Bits and pieces of me, but not the whole me.*
> *I'm hiding here in plain sight. A façade of shoes and hair*
>   *with everything in between camouflaged.*
> *A silent deal I would make for the rest of my life.*
> *These things you can see, the rest are hiding under the tree.*
> *LA*

When Uncle Les died in December 2010, the loss was difficult for me. I never heard him say an unkind word about anyone. He was my designated hitter, filling in for my dad in my life in small ways. When I got married, he lit a candle in the church in memory of my dad. Uncle Leslie told me, "Your dad was the glue that held the family together."

My dad was the fun-loving peacemaker that everyone wanted to be around. He was the typical middle child. When he left high school about three months before graduating to play minor league ball for the Chicago Cubs organization, his mother was distraught.

He was determined to follow in his older brother's footsteps and turn his talent into a job. My dad would spend the next 13 years bouncing through the Cubs' minor league farm system, playing in places such as Lumberton, North Carolina and San Antonio, Texas.

He was a minor-league catcher from 1948-50 and again from 1953-61. It was in 1957 when he got his first taste of managing, serving as player/coach for the Paris, Illinois Lakers in the Class D Midwest League. Perhaps it was no coincidence that was his best season as a player, too, as he hit .321 with 20 home runs.

His dream, of course, was to play in the majors. He never got there. It was his opportunity to manage in the minor leagues that made him realize his best chance to reach the big leagues was as a coach.

In the early 1960s – and really long before that and long after – the Cubs just weren't very good. When they completed the 1960 season with another awful record (60-94), team owner P.K. Wrigley decided enough was enough. That's when the Cubs' innovative, but ill-fated, idea of the "College of Coaches" was born.

In spring training before the 1961 season, based on the advice of Cubs' coach El Tappe, who didn't feel a manager should hire his own coaches, Wrigley appointed a College of Coaches.

It was a rotating team of eight Cubs' coaches, four from the minor-league system and four from the big-league club. The first College of Coaches included Tappe, Goldie Holt, Charlie Grimm, Bobby Adams, Harry Craft, Ripper Collins, Vedie Himsl, and my dad.

Doomed almost from the start, coaches who were tabbed to be the "manager" for a game often received little support from the coaches who weren't managing that game. The experiment was a laughable failure. The team didn't get the jolt Wrigley had hoped for and actually got worse, losing 90 games in 1961 and 103 games in 1962, a team record.

By 1963, the College of Coaches was starting to come apart and by 1965 it was completely abandoned. But my dad had done enough to show the organization that he was worth keeping, and in 1966, new manager Leo Durocher, with significant prodding from the team owner, made my dad his bullpen coach.

The College of Coaches had been a great opportunity for my dad. After all, in 1961 he was 31 years old. While that was approaching middle age for a baseball player, it was just the beginning of a career in coaching.

This was the opportunity he'd been seeking. Just a year earlier he was coaching the Wenatchee, Washington Chiefs and the year before that he was in San Antonio, Texas coaching the San Antonio Missions and the year before that in the middle of downstate Illinois.

He took every job for what it was – a learning experience. Through it all, the big club was paying attention. One Cubs' coach, Bob Kennedy, knew my dad and encouraged Wrigley to choose him as one of the minor-league selections for the College of Coaches. In the end, baseball purists hated it and die-hard Cubs fans were embarrassed by it. There was my father, suspended right in the middle of chaos and criticism. He never complained. He never second-guessed. He never criticized. He did the job he was hired to do.

I will always consider the College of Coaches a beautiful mistake.

Eventually, when Wrigley decided the idea wouldn't work, he designated Bob Kennedy to be the "head" coach of the College of Coaches and that was pretty much the death knell of the idea.

Upon my father's death, he was the only remaining coach from the College of Coaches still on staff for the Cubs. I think that's pretty impressive. Uncle Les told me that my father went to P.K. Wrigley and asked to be named manager but Wrigley said, "Rube, I'd probably have to fire you and I don't want to ever do that."

I share a kinship with some of the daughters of the coaches including Carole Van Matre, the daughter of Harry Craft, and with Chris Mitchell, the daughter of Bob Kennedy. When my story made national headlines they both contacted me through my blog.

In 1961, the College of Coaches was P.K. Wrigley's experiment testing an innovative management approach by having eight coaches take turns calling the shots during games. The experiment failed and was eventually dropped as the Cubs struggled with losing seasons. The eight original men in the College of Coaches were front row, left to right: Elvin Tappe, Goldie Holt, Bobby Adams and Harry Craft; back row, left to right: Verlon Walker, Rip Collins, Vedie Himsl and Charlie Grimm.

Carole referred to us as "kindred baseball spirits." I agree.

She told me a story about the Wrigley's hosting a dinner for the Cubs organization. The dinner invitation stated it would be held "at the stables." The Crafts were from Texas and could not imagine having dinner with horses.

Upon arrival at the Wrigley's stables, Carole wrote that her mother said, "The Wrigley stables were nicer than any home she had ever lived in: controlled air, beautiful brick paved floors and no horse smell."

Carole said she remembered her parents speaking fondly of my dad after they learned of his passing.

Chris Mitchell wrote, "My family remembers your dad so fondly and have great memories of his antics in our backyard." Chris also babysat me during spring training the year my dad went back in the hospital. She told me, "We called the hospital to say goodnight to your dad because you missed him."

During his 11 years as a coach for the Chicago Cubs, Verlon became known as a cultivator of talent, a mentor to young players, and a calm voice of reason in the Durocher dugout.

He must have had a trusted eye for baseball talent because in the off season, the Cubs sent him to Colombia and the Dominican Republic to scout for players.

They called it Winter League ball and I found his passport in one of those old boxes. For the passport picture he is 26 years old, a blue-eyed, brown-haired kid with a listed occupation of "professional ballplayer." He brought my mom tea cups from each place he visited. She still has them displayed in her kitchen. He was a baseball diplomat.

Dad's impact on the team went far beyond the baseball diamond. This became clear in the years after my dad died.

In 1971 the Cubs donated $35,000 to Wesley Memorial Hospital in honor and memory of my father. The donation started the Rube Walker Blood Center at Northwestern University Hospital. This center, which still operates today, is a fitting tribute to a man who spent his life helping others.

Beyond baseball Dad made a difference. He didn't just talk about doing things, he did things. He was a man of action and I liked that.

When he made enough money, he bought two cars; one for himself and one for his mother so she wouldn't have to walk to work anymore. When his mother became ill with ovarian cancer, he took her to Charlotte, North Carolina for the latest cancer treatments. He took charge of the situation by finding and paying for the best care available for his mother.

My dad attended church regularly. One Sunday, after hearing a sermon on the importance of educating the youth, my dad walked up to the minister and handed him $50 and said, "Start a scholarship fund. Here's your first donation."

The minister did just that. The Walker Family Scholarship Fund still exists today, offering scholarships to local students through Trinity United Methodist Church in Lenoir.

Apart from being a man of faith, he enjoyed Early Times Bourbon, classic country music, and stock car racing.

"Mom, what kind of music did my dad like?" I blurted out.

"He liked Merle Haggard. We went to see him in concert in Mesa during spring training," she replied.

I pulled up Merle Haggard on Apple Music as we drove down a long two-lane road edged by open fields. We were on our way to the peach orchard. White peaches, mom's favorite, were in season.

"I liked Willie and he liked Merle," mom laughed.

"We'll listen to Willie next then," I said. "But not *Always on my Mind*. I flat out don't believe a word of that song."

I had found a picture of NASCAR driver Junior Johnson's

1957 Ford in my dad's boxes, so I read Junior's biography. Junior Johnson grew up in Wilkes County in North Carolina. In fact, the Walker family originated in Wilkes County and both families had a history of making and moving moonshine.

Further research revealed that both Merle Haggard and Junior Johnson had both been pardoned by Ronald Reagan for crimes they had committed as young men. Haggard's pardon for a burglary conviction came in 1972 when Reagan was governor of California. Johnson's pardon for a moonshine conviction came in 1986 when Reagan was president. Deductive reasoning: I concluded my father would have liked Ronald Reagan.

I was beginning to see that this was the type of man my dad was: kind, fun-loving, hard-working, mild mannered and charismatic. I had a hunger for him. The only way I knew to satiate myself was get to know him. I was going to do that through baseball.

Dear Dad,
I have missed you. Today I wonder how it might feel to....
  make you laugh
  have you call me on my crap,
  have you take my side
  watch you get frustrated
  hear you say my name
  tell me, "it's going to be OK"
  teach me something
  tell me I'm beautiful
  watch you give a boy the third degree on my behalf
  get mad at me
  look directly in your blue eyes
  watch you walk on the baseball field, notice me in the
  stands, and wink at me
  give me $20.00 for gas

call me

text me

I'm not going to lie, missing you has messed me up. I've spent a lifetime climbing out of the hole you left me in. The most fascinating part is, the closer I get to pulling myself out, the more painful it seems to be. The grief frequency is off the charts.

I have tried so many paths, finally settling on this personal quest to know you and exorcise my demons once and for all.

I thought I would be better by now, like inspiringly "TEDx" better. Instead, here I sit worse than when I began.

In pursuit of you, pieces of me have been burned off. I feel strange. My insides are all twisted. Can you ask the Lord to help me? I can't, I'm pissed at him right now.

Is this one of those "darkest before the dawn" moments? Is this self-induced suffering to which Buddha refers? I have unearthed incredible things while getting to know you. I should feel better.

Can you believe they named a leukemia center at Northwestern Hospital in Chicago after you? The archivist for the hospital, Sue Sacharski, has joined my journey. Her father died the same day you died several years later. We are bound in our March 24th grief. Did you bring her to me? She sent me a package of pictures, press releases, newsletters from the early days of the RUBE WALKER BLOOD CENTER. I am desperate to see the hospital for myself, but I'm afraid to go to the place where you died.

Walker Stadium is not in great shape. I made a passionate plea to a local church to sponsor a banner to hang at Walker Field in honor of Uncle Les near the

memorial for you and Rube. He stayed in Lenoir to
play baseball while ya'll left. There was nothing of
him at Walker Stadium. I thought there should be.
My powers of persuasion worked. A sign hangs in his
honor. Did you do that through me?
How about this...I'm thinking about writing a book
about you. Well, I thought I was writing about you
but it's really about me. I don't know if my journey is
interesting enough, I'm too close to it to tell. Are you
inspiring my writing?
In looking for you, will I finally find myself?
I have no inspiration, no answers.
With an open heart, I step out on faith.
Your daughter,
Leigh Ann

I wrote these letters to help me identify the emotions and where they sat in my body. It was a way for me to bring them up and in a sense, get them out of the way. It was suggested to me by a wise woman that I do this. She said if I communicated with the feelings, it would draw me deeper. She was right.

Journaling was my quiet way of accessing the eternal dialogue. I've cycled in and out of it for many years. I would write in a journal and then stop for a while, rarely going back to read what I had written. Journaling has never pulled me out of a problem. It's something I do in reflective hindsight. Most of it could pass as the ramblings of an unbalanced lunatic, but every now and again when my mind is clear, I tap into just what is happening inside of me. That is where the letters to my father came from.

I've always felt that I'm too sensitive for this world. My journals confirm this.

CHAPTER 2
Those Who Knew Him Best

*M*aybe the best way to describe my journey is to use a situation known to all baseball fans as advancing the runner.

There are many ways to move a runner ahead safely from one base to another. It's not as dramatic as a grand slam, but the goal of baseball is to get the runner on base, move them around and bring them home. It's called "small ball," impacting the game one base at a time. Even if a batter makes an out, he is regarded as having a positive plate appearance, if he advances a runner into scoring position.

The team that advances the runner well has a better chance of winning.

I am the base runner.

Over the course of my journey, I assembled an incredible team to help me advance. My team would play "small ball" by focusing on one stride at a time. They helped me navigate the metaphorical baseball system moving from bush league to major league.

Baseball has no clock, making time irrelevant. I suspended myself in this journey traveling around the bases with my team, at my own pace, and eventually coming home.

I symbolically stepped up to the plate.

Feeling completely removed from the Cubs organization, I just bypassed them altogether. I was intimidated. After all, it had been 40 years since my father had been a part of the team. The organization had changed. Baseball had changed. Most of the people my dad had been involved with were long gone.

I thought my best shot at getting into the Cubs organization was through Chicago-area TV and radio station WGN, which had been the Cubs media outlet in the 1960s. If archives existed, surely WGN would have access.

I sent an email to Pat Hughes, who was the Cubs' play-by-play announcer on WGN. Pat had worked alongside third baseman Ron Santo, revered as one of the great Cubs of all time. After retiring from baseball, Santo became the Cubs' color analyst on WGN with Pat. His effervescence came through every game. When the Cubs won, he celebrated, and when they lost – which was a lot – he commiserated.

My dad was Santo's coach.

Santo played for the Cubs from 1960 to 1973 and suffered through some of the best and worst times the franchise has ever known, but his love and enthusiasm for the Cubs had never wavered. He retired in 1975 after one season with the southside White Sox. Santo often proclaimed himself "the single biggest Cubs fan of all time."

Santo died in December 2010 from a combination of bladder cancer and diabetes which he had suffered with for years. His ashes were spread over his beloved Wrigley Field. He was finally inducted into the Baseball Hall of Fame in 2012 after years of coming up short in voting.

I thought Pat might have known of my dad through Ron. Within a few days of sending my email, much to my surprise, I received an email back from Pat simply saying he would help me. He gave me his phone number. I immediately called him.

It turns out he has daughters and my yearning to know my father struck a chord with him. He didn't know my dad personally but he gave me the names of three people who might be able to help me. I would contact them all.

I would eventually circle back and call the Cubs' front office, but they had no recordings or memorabilia of my dad. It was at this point that I also learned about the cumbersome, expensive reel-to-reel recording process used by radio engineers in the 1960s.

Everything WGN and most other radio stations at the time recorded was on reel-to-reel. The technology was still in its infancy so the TV film and audio tape was recorded over often. That meant WGN had no recordings of my dad. Any pre-or post-game interviews he would have done were erased and reused.

Here's my dad in 1953 in the dugout at one of the minor league stops in his career. Dad learned a little something about baseball from each place he went and by the time he was named as a Chicago Cubs coach, he knew how to mentor young players and be a friend to everyone who worked for the baseball team.

Furthermore, the cassette wasn't widely used until the 1970s, which would make finding a collection of recordings of my dad difficult, if not impossible. He died just before the technology was available.

I'm not going to lie, that was a total letdown. I thought once I got through to WGN, they would open their archives to me and behold, I would see and hear my father. I realized then that this journey would not be short or simple. I was being forced to accept the limitations of the time period and the fact that I might have waited too long to get started.

My hope had been that through grainy video or scratchy audio, I might be able to see the way he walked, hear his voice, watch him interact, see his hands move, his facial expressions. With technological help, I would be able to see if there was anything of him in me. It is something most people take for granted – the knowledge of a person's presence.

If you close your eyes right now you can probably see and hear a lost loved one. You can hear a particular moment that represents their personality or see them in a place that meant so much to them. You can call upon your history with them to know what advice they might give you in a present situation. You can remember what their hand felt like when you grabbed it and whether it was soft or cold, callused, sweaty.

But I had no history or memory of such things. Everything was new to me.

At this point I made a conscious decision to allow the journey to take me wherever it led. Like the current of a river, I was going to trust the flow to carry me where I needed to go. Maybe it had someplace truly wonderful and unexpected to take me. I would pursue any and all leads, believing that each one had come to me for a reason with something to contribute.

Pat Hughes had given me the email address of George Castle,

an accomplished Chicago journalist and baseball historian, and an author of 14 books. I figured I may as well ask him for advice.

I sent him a detailed email. Within hours, I had a response. He wanted to talk to me, write a story about me, and put me in touch with players who knew my dad. He was going to help.

George became my confidant, my voice of reason, my mentor, my team manager. He helped me broaden my quest by saying "talk to the guys that knew your dad. They will give you his voice."

He gave me a list of names of players to contact. I stared at the list for days feeling myself slipping back into the painfully shy little girl who only felt comfortable sitting silent next to her mother.

George would say things to urge me forward like, "Carolina Girl, your dad would be proud of you. Now get to work!"

I was uncomfortable and a bit nervous.

There I was with my list, sitting at my computer, phone in hand, perched at the razor's edge of my fear. I practiced, "Hi, my name is Leigh Ann. My father was Verlon Walker and he was a coach for the Cubs when you were a player. Do you remember him?"

I breathed bravery into each word until I felt I could say it without bursting into tears. It felt emotionally dangerous to reach out to strangers in such a vulnerable way. I was exposing that wound I had spent a lifetime hiding.

Ferguson Jenkins, Cubs pitcher and Hall of Famer, is one of the most beloved players in team history. He was the first player I called. I had a picture of him with my dad at a Cubs convention the year before Dad died. I felt sure he would remember my dad.

Ferguson, known as Fergie to all Cubs fans, had played a total of 10 seasons for the Cubs (1966-73 and again at the end of his career in 1982-83). He is still the team leader in strikeouts with 2,038 and fifth all-time in victories with 167. His number

31 has been retired by the team and he was inducted into the Hall of Fame in 1991.

I didn't look any of that up before I called. Thank goodness or I would have been really nervous.

The phone rang and he answered.

"Hi, Mr. Jenkins. You don't know me. My name is Leigh Ann and my dad, Verlon Walker, was a coach for the Cubs when you were a player. Do you remember him?"

I said it just as I had practiced it. As it turned out, that's also all I could say before the lump in my throat dislodged and melted into tears. I held my breath and swallowed hoping to force the lump down instead.

Then came his response.

"I do remember him," Fergie said. "He was a true gentleman. A kind man."

Fergie's voice was soft and sympathetic.

I told him I was looking for information about my dad. He asked, "How old were you when he died?"

"Three…I was three," I replied.

Despite my best efforts to be in the moment, emotionless and just listening, my eyes burned. I exhaled and began to cry.

"I remember him helping the younger guys with batting practice. He was a nice guy," Fergie offered up.

"OK, thank you so much for taking the time to talk to me. I hope I didn't bother you."

I was scarcely able to speak. I was pathetically raw and unprepared.

What the hell?

I had started crying and practically hung up on Ferguson Jenkins!

I didn't prepare a list of questions. I didn't record the conversation. I didn't anticipate that much emotion. I didn't realize just how shattered I was. I had touched something that completely overwhelmed me. My reaction to that split-second connection to my dad revealed my wound.

My emotional lifeguard threw me a lifeline and an impressive glaze of numbness came over me. Just like that, I was back to normal and the tears stopped. I felt nothing. I enmeshed myself in my daily chores of laundry, grocery shopping, carpool at my kids' school. Continuing through my day as if nothing had happened, I made dinner, did the dishes, helped my son with his homework, took a bath and went to bed. I didn't allow myself to feel any of it.

For weeks, I walked around vacillating between awareness and numbness. I saw right then how my detachment had helped me survive. I was terrified to feel the grief and loss. But if I was going to take this journey, I would have to.

So, as I found myself doing often during my journey, I faced those issues head on and sent a direct appeal to, in this case, the numbness I felt afterward.

> *Dear Numbness,*
> *Thank you. I have survived because of you. When I*
> *summon, you rush forth.*
> *I feel you enter behind my eyes, slide down my neck,*
> *cascading like waterfalls over the front and back of*
> *my shoulder, soaking my heart and lungs, swirling*
> *through my stomach and settling in my hips.*
> *You feel amazing. Better than any drug. You are my*
> *vehicle to dissociation.*
> *I walk around in a senseless, disinterested stupor.*
> *You are the reason I need to constantly ask myself, "how do*
> *I really feel about this?" I don't know anymore.*
> *This is where I have to leave you. I'll miss your consistent*

companionship, but if I'm going to find my father, you
can't come.
    LA

There is a part of me stranded on the road where my dad left me. I am still the little girl who never progressed past the loss.

I've lived my life through that little girl's eyes, tip-toeing around the hurt. Talking with Fergie Jenkins transformed me immediately into that little stranded girl. If I had had a list of questions prepared, I wouldn't have been able to speak them. That phone call had ripped the bandage off my wound.

It took me a while, but the next person I contacted was Joey Amalfitano. When I was in middle school, Joey had sent me a letter and a picture of himself in a Los Angeles Dodgers uniform.

His letter explained how he had been a player when my dad was a coach for the Cubs. He hoped I was well. I put the color photograph up in my bedroom until one of my friends came over and asked me, "Who is that?"

"He used to play baseball with my dad," I answered.

My friend was shocked.

"Your dad played professional baseball?" she asked.

A barrage of questions followed which I didn't want to answer. What team did he play for? Did you live in Chicago? He died? How did he die? Do you miss him?

"Chicago Cubs. I don't remember living in Chicago. I was only 2 years old. He died of leukemia. I don't miss him."

All my answers were true. I didn't miss him. I never knew him, so how could I?

When she left, I put the picture away and honestly don't know what happened to it. It's possible I threw it away. I found that by controlling the narrative, I could manage my emotions. Out of sight. Out of mind. A plan I implemented for the rest of my life. I did write Joey a thank you note but I never heard from him again.

I googled "Joey Amalfitano" and learned he was now a scout for the San Francisco Giants. Coincidentally, George Castle had given me the email address of the public relations director for the Giants. I sent him my contact information and asked that it be passed along to Joey.

Within days I got a call.

Walking out of a late evening yoga class, I looked at my phone. I had a voice message from a strange number, "Wow, Leigh Ann Walker! It's been a long time since I saw you, young lady."

It was Joey.

I sat down on a bench in the dark outside the yoga studio. In a sweaty haze, I listened to the voice message several times. The night air chilled me. I knew I wasn't prepared to talk to him after I had cried with Fergie, but I was so curious to hear what he had to say. I stood up, walked to my car slowly and hit "call back". Joey answered.

"Hey, it's Leigh Ann. Thank you so much for calling me. How are you?"

"Hello, dear. The question is, how are you?" he said.

I spent a few minutes telling him about my life in Charlotte and my quest to learn about my dad.

"Your dad was a good coach, a good friend and, boy, did he love you," he said.

"I don't remember him," I interjected.

"Girl, you were the joy of his world. He would carry you around the field before the games showing you off," Joey said.

He laughed, replaying it in his mind as if it had happened only last week.

Joey told me Leo Durocher was forced by P.K. Wrigley to keep my dad on staff referring to my dad as a "house guy."

This immediately put him at odds with Leo. Somehow, my dad managed to win over the volatile Durocher.

Joey added, "Leo respected your dad's opinion. He would ask him to weigh in on decisions. Leo listened to your dad."

Now I knew how my dad had survived as a coach for 11 years. He had endeared himself to both Wrigley and Durocher. I learned once again that my dad was well respected in baseball circles for his baseball knowledge, and perhaps more importantly for his friendly demeanor that endeared him to just about everyone.

While the Durocher information was interesting, I couldn't shake the image of my dad carrying me around Wrigley Field.

I have a picture of Yogi Berra carrying me around Wrigley, my uncle Rube carrying me around Wrigley and me sitting on my dad's lap next to the third base brick wall at Wrigley Field. I was there, but I have no memory of it.

Joey and I talked for about 15 minutes. I ended up crying, which made both of us a bit uncomfortable. I was sitting in a dark parking lot in sweaty yoga clothes, but the only sensations I felt were internal. My insides were a stirred-up mix of excitement and sorrow. I whispered to myself, "You have to remember this."

I could feel it slipping away from me. I had spent a lifetime not remembering and going numb. I had always counted on the instinct to go numb, detach from the story and just forget. I had no paper and no pen so I turned on the video camera on my phone and spoke all I could remember.

Driving home, I decided I needed to establish some structure around these interviews. I couldn't just call these people seeking information and not have a plan. I couldn't collapse into an emotional wreck after each conversation. I was in a street fight with the part of me that had spent a lifetime not attaching to these stories. I was not going to go numb anymore.

I made a plan. I would buy a notebook and write down a few questions before I made another call. If I was prepared, like a journalist, I could get in front of the emotion. I would practice.

This was my absurd attempt to manage a raging storm of grief that was nauseatingly close to the surface. I had no idea what I was dealing with and just how quickly it would undo me.

I emailed Don Kessinger, the Cubs shortstop from 1964 to 1975, asking if he remembered my dad and if he knew anyone who might have audio or video of him. Email felt safe.

Kessinger was another of those beloved Cubs who played at a time when the team went through its share of valleys and mountains. He was a six-time All-Star and the reliable shortstop who won Gold Gloves in 1969 and 1970.

Don responded within a few days:

> Leigh Ann,
> It is so great to hear from Verlon Walker's daughter. Your dad was one of the nicest men I was around in baseball. I am sorry I do not have anything that would help you in your search. You have contacted the people I thought might have something. This email brought back some really fond memories of the years your dad coached and I played.
> Don Kessinger

I couldn't believe how quickly people were responding to me. I decided to take a few hours each week to focus on my quest. I would make calls, ask my questions, write it all down and document what I found on a blog. It would be a way for me to keep track of what I was finding, legitimizing my efforts at the same time.

My next call was to Jack Rosenburg, the retired sports editor for WGN. I had my notebook but no questions. I planned to let him talk, take notes and ask questions based on what he said. I just didn't know what to ask except, "Do you remember my dad?" Plus, I had this self-defeating belief that I was bothering people.

Jack did remember him.

"Your father was consistently nice. A man of character," he said. Jack never witnessed my dad angry or frustrated. Because he was in the media, Jack had the opportunity to see players and coaches on a regular basis and saw how they reacted to wins and losses.

"Baseball was different back then," he said. "Sports writers had more contact with the players and coaches. Your father was in the bullpen a lot working with the young guys. I remember that."

Jack was the first person to give me the image of my dad as a teacher of young players.

I held that image of him in my mind. An even-tempered mentor who I could see working in the bullpen with young pitchers. I imagined he was a great teacher and I imagined the young pitchers hung on his every word. After all, in his playing days he'd been a catcher and would have a deep understanding of the pitcher.

Joey Amalfitano told me Durocher respected my dad's advice and now I'm learning that he was respected by the young guys, too. I couldn't help but think how much I needed my dad's wise words and his spotlight of attention.

Then it hit me like a line drive to the temple – my life would have been so much better with Dad to guide me.

I had always assumed it, but now I had proof. Dad would have treated me the way he treated other people. I would have flourished. With him guiding me I wouldn't have been such a foolish, defiant girl with a long list of bad decisions.

My conclusion after talking with Jack was that God did this. He took my father.

I was seething. The next morning when I dropped Christopher, my youngest child, at the Baptist Church Preschool, I was handed a flyer proclaiming the "Good News!" an Easter Extravaganza celebrating the Father, the Son and the Holy Spirit that weekend.

I took the flyer and stuffed it in the garbage can outside the church, mumbling to myself, "They can all three kiss my ass! The Father, the Son and the Holy Spirit." It was unjust.

Dear Father, Son and Holy Spirit,
Confession: I'm pissed. Enraged even
The blood and bandages of suffering passed off as the
*   sweeping hand of God's will, unfolding for the*
*   greater good.*
(insert eye roll with huge sigh here)
I just can't.
You have messengers down here intervening on your
*   behalf, feeding me mumbo-jumbo, hocus-pocus,*
*   double talk.*
Here's a sampling,
The Lord took your father so you could draw closer to him.
He was such a good man that God needed him in heaven
*   to be an angel.*
It was God's will and we don't always understand God's
*   will.*
You will get to be with him in heaven one day.
And my personal favorite…
God gave you your own guardian angel.
I don't believe a word of it anymore and I'm tired of being
*   polite about it.*
Save the non-sense for the simpletons
This is where I leave you….
LA

Outwardly, I pretended I wasn't angry, busying myself with my daily life and snapping on my game face. This wasn't the first time I had been irate with God, but this time I was a grown woman. The anger felt cumulative, electric, permanent. My surrender and acceptance absconded in the night and left me with rage. I was energized by it.

This was a productive time. I researched players that my dad coached, making lists of the ones who were still alive. I plotted how I would track them down. It's funny, as terrified as I had originally been in trying to ask these former players and coaches about my dad, I found I was growing more comfortable.

I had been out of control with grief when I began but the more I did it, the less the tears came. I found that people I contacted to talk to were not mean to me. They were happy to talk about my father and, in some cases, they provided answers to questions I never even asked. I really felt I was loved all through it. The people made it easier and much of the fear of being rejected was eliminated.

I had a picture of my dad with Sandy Koufax. I began trying to contact the very private former Dodgers pitcher. I never did get an interview with Sandy, but I did talk to someone who knows him. I was one degree of separation from "the man with the golden arm."

My determination was driven by my anger. I watched Ken Burns' entire documentary on baseball. I made a timeline of my dad's baseball career and laminated it at Kinko's. I played baseball with my kids in the backyard until dark. The anger didn't seem to dissipate, but grew stronger.

I continued on.

Dick Ellsworth, Cubs pitcher from 1960 to 1965, remembered my dad's quiet sense of humor and dry wit. His wife played him the voicemail I left and he made a special trip home to call me back.

"Your dad was always early at the ballpark like myself," Dick said. "He asked me one day, 'Lefty, why do you get here so early?' I told him, 'I can't wait to put this uniform on.' Your father said, 'Me neither.'"

"What do you remember about him?" I asked.

Dick paused before he answered, "Integrity. Everyone liked him because of his integrity. He didn't get involved in the politics of baseball. He just loved the game. He was one of the good guys."

I talked with Dick for about 20 minutes. When we hung up I was full of joy. My father was a man of integrity. He was grateful. He got paid to play a game. Baseball had lifted him out of poverty.

Next I called Chris Krug, a Cubs catcher from 1965 to 1967. After retiring from baseball, Chris returned to college in his home town of Los Angeles and became a landscape artist. He started his own landscape company and eventually wound up designing the ball diamond in the Iowa cornfield made famous in Kevin Costner's film *Field of Dreams*. I've been in love with Kevin Costner since he played Crash Davis in the movie *Bull Durham* and delivered the line "I believe in long, slow, deep, soft wet kisses that last for three days."

I sat on my front porch one afternoon while my kids played in the yard and called Chris Krug.

"Chris, my name is Leigh Ann Walker. I'm Verlon Walker's daughter. Do you remember my dad?"

"He was my coach!" Chris responded.

No hesitation. No waffling. He recalled the memory of my father right then and there. "He was my coach!"

He told me the story of how one day he was sitting alone in the dugout pensively thinking about the status of his contract with the team. My dad came and sat down next to him, sensing he was worried about his standing with the club. He said my dad's advice was simple and direct, which, as I was learning, was typical of my father.

"You are our catcher now," Verlon Walker, the coach, told the young Chris. "Focus on that and enjoy this time."

As it turned out, Leo Durocher did indeed replace Chris the next season with Randy Hundley. But 40 years later Chris had not forgotten my father's kindness and advice.

I think my dad would have liked Chris' initial response, "He was my coach!" People remember the way you make them feel, and it was clear my father's legacy of kindness had remained with Chris all these years.

I had fun talking to Chris Krug. He was just what I needed. I had been approaching this quest with such heavy sadness that had turned to anger. Chris made me laugh. He loosened me up a little. I began to understand that this discovery process didn't have to be a slog through grief. It could be enjoyable.

My next contact was Bill Hands, who pitched for the Cubs from 1966 to 1972 coming to the Cubs with Leo Durocher. I called him one evening.

"Mr. Hands, my name is Leigh Ann Walker. I am the daughter of Verlon Walker who was a coach when you were a player for the Cubs. Do you remember him?"

"Of course, I remember him! Do you still live in Lenoir?" Bill said.

I was blown away. After all these years, this man remembered the strange name of my dad's hometown with perfect recall.

"No, I live in Charlotte. It's about an hour and a half away, but my mom still lives there," I said.

"Your dad told me my dining room table was probably made in Lenoir because that's where all the nice furniture was made," he said with a laugh. "He loved his hometown. Talked about it like crazy. We were all tired of hearing about that place."

He laughed again.

"Yes, I have been told he talked Lenoir up and I'm sure he was right about your dining table," I said, "but only if it was pretty."

"Oh, you got your dad's wit," Bill said.

That stopped me cold. I'm witty? My dad was witty. That was evidence of him in me. I started to become more aware of my humor. It was the first time that I realized, in my quest for him, I was also looking for myself.

Bill was the first person to mention leukemia. He said my dad had confided in him about his diagnosis. "It was sad. He was a humble man. He didn't have a mean bone in his body," he said.

Bill recalled one evening they were in the locker room together after a game. Most people had left and my dad pulled up his shirt to reveal his back, asking Bill if he could see any marks. Bill confirmed there were blue spots on his back and on his sides.

People with leukemia commonly have bruises that show up in strange places like the back. I didn't know this until Bill mentioned it. While looking at images of leukemia bruises, I thought about how difficult it must have been for my dad, as an athlete, to have his body react this way – to turn on him.

I also read that leukemia would have made him exhausted and weak. He would have lost weight and been susceptible to infections and had a difficult time fighting them off. Nose bleeds, night sweats and these bruises that Bill mentioned were part of his battle fighting against leukemia.

I understand why he kept his illness to himself. That's what I would do. I wouldn't want my disease to become the focus with people I worked with. I wouldn't want to politely answer questions about it and I wouldn't want people to feel sorry for me.

I had sent pitcher Ken Holtzman an email because George Castle had suggested it. Ken pitched a no-hitter at Wrigley Field on August 19, 1968, and my mom and I were in attendance at the game. I was only 4 months old.

One morning I woke up to his email response:

> I do indeed have fond memories of your father. He was a coach in the Cubs system when I came up and was very helpful to young players like me. He was ordinarily a quiet, reserved person but was also super competitive and we used to enjoy the back and forth banter with his brother on the Mets. I know you were very young when he passed, but I'm glad you're seeking out the memories of his life. My grandkids do the same to me and it is a way of connecting families through the generations. I hope you reach many players and that they enrich your father's memory. With best wishes,
> Ken Holtzman
> PS – He always used to brag about Lenoir!

I am trying to connect generations, too. I wanted to know my dad so I could give him to my sons.

My oldest son Walker is a natural athlete with zero interest in playing baseball. He bats left and throws right, just like my dad. I've spent hours in the backyard throwing baseballs to him. Somewhere around the fourth grade his hitting skills surpassed my pitching skills. It was downright dangerous for me to stand out there. His temperament is polite and easy going. Walker is grounded, level headed and cool. I have learned from listening to his pragmatic views of life.

My youngest, Christopher, is also a natural hitter with little interest in the game. He bats right handed but does most everything else left-handed. His temperament reminds me of

Uncle Leslie. He is passionate, loyal, and certain; Christopher is ruled by his heart. Unburdened by time, he lives in the moment with his emotions. He loves deeply and is capable of intense fits of anger. From him, I have learned to be in the moment and connect to my feelings.

My sons have completely different personalities. They came through me into this world, unique and with great purpose; just as I came through my dad. We bring pieces of past generations with us into present day. There is something of my dad in my sons. I started looking for that, too.

They both have a general understanding of what I have embarked on and refer to me as "mama strong." I'm not just strong, I'm mama strong. They have watched me confront my fears and fire walk through them. They have supported me, but I have purposely not forced this on them. This is my journey and they will benefit as I share what I learn through love and a playful spirit.

It doesn't bother me that Walker and Christopher have little interest in baseball. I'm sure if my father had been present in their lives, he would have given them what I couldn't. They would have also had another example of integrity and unconditional love in their lives. Walker and Christopher have a unique path to walk that doesn't include baseball. That's OK with me because they are their own people and that's as it should be. I can't wait to see what they do.

After having some success with interviews and emails with players, I decided to approach collectors and Cubs fans. They might have stories, pictures, or a recording of my dad. I needed to get my story out there to reach them, so I launched my own PR campaign. I reached out to newspapers, magazines, blogs, sports radio, asking if they would promote my story. It was a risk, a shot in the dark, but I approached it with an idealistic, wide-eyed innocence. Just like a little girl in search of her father.

The media embraced me. I got more publicity than I was prepared for, including a segment on Keith Olbermann's ESPN show. The Olbermann spotlight was a watershed moment. He told my story with such emotion and I received an outpouring of well-wishes and leads.

I was featured in articles by the Associated Press, *The Chicago Tribune*, *Bleed Cubbie Blue*, *The Charlotte Observer* and several collector's magazines. I was a guest on talk radio shows and podcasts. Doing interviews, like my father used to do, the very ones I was searching for. I had come full circle. I had become his voice, promoting his legacy.

Emails continued to come. Former major league catcher Terry Kennedy and the son of Bob Kennedy, sent me this:

Leigh Ann,

My name is Terry Kennedy. I am a former major league player and son of Bob Kennedy. My dad was manager when your father was coach with the Cubs. I remember your father well even though I was only 8 years old. You don't forget someone that nice. My father was a good judge of character and he loved your dad.

I remember when I would go on the field in my own little flannel Cubs uniform and play catch with whoever was out there. I threw a few with your dad. Now, my father is gone, too. It doesn't matter what age you are, there is always loss (I was 49 when he passed). I have followed your quest and wish you well. I have seen the list of sources you have tried and I cannot think of anymore that I could suggest. I was sure WGN would have something.

I will pray for you in your search and as one baseball kid to another, I understand. Perhaps, as you have mentioned, it's not the prize but the journey that will fulfill your dream.

God Bless,

Terry Kennedy

I was stuck on "you don't forget someone that nice." I read the email over and over. People from the past were showing up for my dad, bestowing me with the same kindness he had shown them. Terry was right, the journey was healing me. I was cycling through all sorts of emotions. By this point, I reached an excited satisfaction.

Bob Kennedy's daughter Chris Mitchell sent me this email:

Your Dad was one of the nicest men our family knew. He was funny and a lot of fun whenever he came over to our house. We knew him before he married your mother. One fact you may not remember is that I babysat you during spring training the year your Dad went back in the hospital. In fact, the doctor called with test results while your parents were out to dinner and I took the message. Once, while caring for you, we called the hospital to say goodnight to your Dad because you were so upset he wasn't home. My family remembers him so fondly and have great memories of his antics in our back yard.

I hope you are successful in your search.

Chris (Kennedy) Mitchell

I clearly had a connection to my father as a little girl. I wanted to talk to him in the hospital because he wasn't home. I have no memory of him, but he was registered somewhere in my heart. I had known him once and missed him and cried until my babysitter called the hospital so I could tell him good night.

After all this national attention on my story, journalists and collectors began searching for pieces of my dad on my behalf all over the country.

I called a collector in Mesa, Arizona, where the Cubs spring training was located and introduced myself. He informed me that he had already been contacted by a gentleman regarding Verlon "Rube" Walker. My team reached beyond the visible players on my roster.

I received emails from strangers "who had a friend who knew a collector who might have a story about my dad." I honored each contact that came my way. Many times, they led only to a pleasant conversation about the golden age of baseball. Yet, every exchange gave me something.

I received a long, detailed email from a baseball fan who came across my story in the *Chicago Tribune*. He wrote about listening to the games on the radio as a boy. His phone number was at the bottom of the email so I called him. He didn't remember my father, but from him I learned about the changing strike zone in major league baseball in the 1960s.

In 1961 Roger Maris broke Babe Ruth's home run record. This didn't sit well with some fans of "The Babe." By 1963 the strike zone was enlarged to give the pitcher more advantage over the hitter. In baseball, there is a "rectangle of power" hovering over home plate called the strike zone. Shrink the rectangle and the advantage goes to the hitter; enlarge the rectangle and the advantage goes to the pitcher.

By 1968, the pitchers dominated the game and created a problem. Fans came to games to see hits. So when batting averages started to sink, so did attendance around the league.

The following year the strike zone was shrunk. My dad had a front row seat to it all. As a former catcher and a soon to be pitching coach, I pondered what his reaction would be to the change.

Letting any information about baseball, my dad, or myself, settle in my bones was quietly powerful. I needed to welcome the words in and sit with them until they became part of me.

Laying in my bed at night, I would close my eyes and imagine him walking toward me. Smiling, like he was glad to see me. I anticipated an embrace. In first person, I saw him through my eyes, pulling him closer to me. I reached out for him, but like a mirage, he would vanish. I would start the vision over again and again until I fell asleep. I took it as an omen to continue and was hopeful that he would eventually walk all the way to me if I did.

Each conversation was building on the one before and leading to the next like an elaborate puzzle. The quest had taken me in directions I hadn't anticipated and through emotions I didn't know were in me.

It was becoming clear that my dad had impacted the lives of so many people over the years. Whether it was a Hall of Famer like Fergie Jenkins or a journeyman catcher like Chris Krug who remembered my dad so vividly for his well-placed and badly needed advice. Players, famous and otherwise, had remembered my dad and, perhaps more important, truly liked him and missed him.

Another Cubs' Hall of Famer embraced my dad. Ernie Banks, famous for his child-like love of the game. He is known for having said, "Let's Play Two!" It was a simple acknowledgement that the only thing better than playing one baseball game is playing yet another one.

Ernie Banks played for the Cubs from 1953-71 and he still owns many Cubs' records including games played (2,528), at-bats (9,421), extra base hits (1,009) and total bases (4,706). He also hit 512 home runs and drove in 1,636 runs. His iconic No. 14 was the first number ever retired by the franchise.

There was also one other record Banks held. The 2,528 games he played is still a record for the most games played without a postseason appearance.

Banks, an accomplished shortstop and later a first baseman, had opportunities to sign with other teams that had a better chance than the Cubs to reach the playoffs, but Banks remained a Cub. He died in 2015 and was mourned by baseball fans everywhere.

In his heyday with the Cubs, Banks wrote a weekly column for the *Chicago Tribune*. One column actually focused on my dad.

Who is Verlon (Rube) Walker?

He's that funny guy I want to tell you about. He is as droll as Will Rogers, and almost every day he comes up with a wisecrack that helps ease the tension of a long season.

There are two Rube Walkers. Rube I, whose first name is Al, was a Cubs catcher a few years before I came up in 1953 and later played for the Dodgers. He is now the pitching coach of the New York Mets.

Verlon, or Rube II, never played a game in the big leagues. He was a catcher in such places as Lumberton, Topeka, Macon, Des Moines, Wenatchee, San Antonio, Pueblo, Sioux Falls and Paris, Texas.

Banks went on talk a little about where Dad came from and how much he loved his hometown of Lenoir. Banks then talked about my dad's dry sense of humor.

The other night in Atlanta when Willie Smith hit the longest major league homer in the new stadium, Rube said: "If Willie had hit that one in our park in

Lenoir, three outfielders would have raced in to make the catch."

The Astrodome? Rube says there are several of them in Lenoir that are known as beehives. The John Hancock building, he says would look no bigger than a telephone booth in his home town.

The National and American Leagues have tried for years, he says, to talk Lenoir into accepting a franchise, "We have a fine team in Lenoir," says Rube, "and wouldn't want to lower the class of baseball there.'

I'll have to visit Lenoir one of these days.

When (third base coach Pete) Reiser is taking it easy, Rube's our quarterback in the third base coaching box. He can give you a quick analysis of any player in the majors – what he can do or cannot do, how fast he is, how well he throws, and how good his stamina is.

Come to think of it, maybe Rube Walker makes all those wisecracks to make us forget about all the punishment we take from the drivers of this team.

Mom told me that Ernie and my dad were friends. I sent an email to Ernie's personal assistant, Regina Rice, the year before he died asking Ernie to contact me. She responded with "thank you for the email." I never heard from Ernie.

Then came a major breakthrough.

My mom had contacted a local minister, Joe Parker, about my desire to hear my father's voice. Joe Parker knew my father well. He was the minister at South Lenoir Methodist Church where the Walker family attended. Joe remembered that my father had invited Bobby Richardson, the New York Yankees second baseman and fellow Southerner, to speak at South Lenoir Methodist Church in 1966.

This service was broadcast on WJRI, Lenoir's local AM radio station. Joe had a recording of it. My mother had it transferred to a CD. On the recording my father introduces Bobby Richardson. His speech lasts about 90 seconds. It's also available on YouTube if you'd like to listen.

I wasn't sure what to make of it. His voice wasn't as deep as I had imagined. His accent was familiar, like my uncles'. He seemed nervous speaking in front of the church congregation.

It was a remarkable step forward to hear that voice.

I tried to imagine him saying my name. I incorporated it into my visons of him walking toward me, smiling at me, saying my name. I just couldn't quite hear it though. I couldn't make it transfer to my mirage.

I needed more time and information. I was thawing out slowly, letting my dad in piece by piece. Like digesting food, I could only take in so much until I was full. I needed to absorb what I collected.

My team had advanced me home. I had scored, but there was more baseball to play.

> *Dear Dad,*
> *I'm way more hurt by your absence than I realized.*
> *I started something, I'm not sure I can handle. I've done all this in pursuit of you. To get to know you.*
> *Are you amazed at how your friends remember you so vividly after all these years? They have all been so nice to me.*
> *I'm learning how to talk about you with an open heart.*
> *LA*
> *P.S. I'm mad at God. I acted ugly at the Baptist church and I'm not sorry.*

CHAPTER 3
What's In a Name

*L*earning about the man named Rube Walker was made a little more difficult because my famous uncle and father shared that same unusual nickname.

Rube? Really?

My uncle, Albert Bluford Walker, born on May 16, 1926, was the oldest Walker boy. I knew him as "Uncle Rube."

He got the nickname, or so I'm told, from the days when he was batboy for the local team in the Class D North Carolina State League. His idol was the star of the team, Rube Robinson. I guess he just adopted the name, too.

The definition of "rube," according to the dictionary, is "a country bumpkin, an awkward, unsophisticated person." I don't think my dad or uncle fit that definition. Jokingly, maybe, but that was all.

They were country boys with a bootlegging heritage. And they were not typical of a lot of kids in those days. They were sons of a factory worker and were not particularly interested in education. They left school to pursue baseball and they were both successful. They were successful rubes.

When I set about recreating my father in my mind, I

kept running into the issue of their shared nickname. Most people who refer to Rube Walker are talking about my uncle. I've had many phone calls that ended with me explaining the brothers Rube and how the information they had so graciously provided me was about my uncle, not my father. It was fine. I would learn about them both.

Before my quest, I didn't know how my uncle got the nickname "Rube," or that he won the World Series as a coach for the 1969 New York Mets. I didn't know that he was on a team with Jackie Robinson, that he instituted the five-man pitching rotation or that he was playing golf with Gil Hodges the day the Hall of Fame first baseman and beloved manager of the Mets died of a heart attack.

I only knew him as my uncle, my dead father's brother. When he visited me, we would talk about me and his daughters, Barbie, Debbie and Janet.

I was the youngest of the girls. Uncle Rube's youngest daughter, Janet, and I played together as kids. Barbie, the middle daughter, lived close by visiting me the most often as I grew up. Debbie, the oldest, I have only seen once that I remember. I have reconnected with them all as a result of this journey.

Barbie Walker Belas wrote to me saying, "Leigh, you have travelled down a road many have not gone. You have shared your journey with others which is very hard to do! You have opened your heart which is a powerful thing; through you others can realize they are not alone and that takes a special person."

I asked her to tell me what she remembered about my dad.

"To me your dad had the coolest cars. He would come by our house and would pick one of us up and take us to Grandma and Grandpa Walker's house.

"One night your dad showed up at our house on South Main Street and it was late. He said it was snowing in Boone.

We were all excited, so we climbed into his Jeep. We were going snow hunting! We went and picked up Uncle Les. We drove up to Boone and guess what? No snow. It was cold and the wind was roaring. We even drove around awhile looking for snow. It would have been great to see some, but the time we all had together laughing was a lot sweeter.

"I always loved when Uncle Verlon came to town. Your dad came to visit after we moved to Maryland. I would sing around the house and make up my own songs. My mom insisted I sing for your dad. Of course, I sounded like a screaming chicken but you would never know by looking at his face. Even though I sounded awful, your dad made me feel like a superstar. In fact, all the Walker brothers had a way about them that made you feel special. Criticism was not in their vocabulary."

The Walker boys pose during a 1969 regular-season series in Chicago. My dad was a third base coach for the Cubs and Uncle Rube was a pitching coach for the New York Mets. The two teams battled for the National League East title that year and were it not for a Cubs late-season collapse, my dad would have had the best of my uncle. But it never quite worked out. Funny thing is, the two men never really talked about what happened that season. (Photo courtesy of Leslie Walker)

69

She went on to discuss her dad, Rube:

"When my sisters and I participated in any type of athletic program or sporting event Dad would see how the coach interacted with the team. He was very particular how we would be coached. He believed that the number one rule was to have fun. He did not want anything to get in the way of the love we had for that particular sport. He wanted us to keep the perspective and not get stressed over a game. If he disagreed with the coaching style, we were not to play. When I started coaching I asked him for advice. Dad told me, 'Everyone is to have fun. Everyone is going to play, and everyone is going to be supportive.'"

Uncle Rube's youngest daughter, Janet Walker Dziesinki, remembers riding in my dad's Jeep when she was three years old.

"One particular time, he bought me cowboy boots. When we got back to Grandma Walker's your Dad said, 'Hey Janet, you go in and tell Grandma Walker we've been out drinking beer all day.' Grandma yelled, 'Verlon Walker, don't teach this baby those things.'

"Your dad had a smile that would make anyone smile back. He loved life and had a great sense of humor," Janet continued. "My dad had a kind heart and he was very responsible. He was the most thoughtful man I have ever known. He spent lots of time with us in the off season and that was priceless. He really didn't complain at all. He loved his work and knew it well."

In the 20 years after my father's death until his death in 1992, I didn't see Uncle Rube much. His life was in baseball and mine was in Lenoir. Our paths just didn't cross.

Maybe it was just too painful for him to think about his brother. I'm sure that was part of it. I think we all wanted to pretend we were fine. Everyone handles grief differently. My family just didn't talk about it. They took it to God in silence.

As a grown woman, I wish I could talk to my uncle now. He could answer so many of my questions.

I did attend several Atlanta Braves games when Uncle Rube was the pitching coach there. I watched him walk around the field. His shoulders rolled a bit forward, his hands brushing against the side of his thighs as they slowly swayed forward and back in rhythm with his feet. I bet my dad walked like that. I fantasized briefly that he was my dad and I was in the stands visiting him that day. My imagination was vivid. If I needed to retreat there, I could on command.

I went to Uncle Rube at the wall near the dugout before the game. It was tradition. Walking down the concrete stadium stairs looking at him looking at me, I felt myself tearing up.

I paused and glanced into the crowd as a distraction to shake me out of my sad yearning. All I needed was a quick second, a few breaths and I could withdraw. My sadness blocker worked every time. I was actually impressed at how quickly I could go numb and be what I thought everyone expected. I was suddenly a happy girl, ready for some baseball.

"Leigh," Uncle Rube called out, "You like your seats?" My seats were always behind the backstop. A prime location to see a baseball game. Also, optimal for people like me who didn't always pay attention and the backstop was protection from rogue baseballs.

"Of course! You gonna win today?" I replied.

"I hope so. It's all Bedrock," he said, referring to Steve Bedrosian, the pitcher with the unusual nickname.

He handed me an autographed baseball that I put it in my bag. I just sat there for a while taking it all in. I waited for him to reach for my hand. When he did, I squeezed it hard and brought it to my lips and kissed it. Then I pressed the back of his hand to my check and held it there. He felt sorry for me; I could see it in his eyes. We said nothing and I returned to my seat.

We always had short visits. I cherished each one, but there were things I didn't know about him either. I decided to find out all I could about Uncle Rube, too.

Al "Rube" Walker, paved the way into baseball for my father by showing him that a boy from nowhere could follow his dream to somewhere.

He started his career with the Chicago Cubs in 1948 but was traded to the Brooklyn Dodgers on June 15, 1951, along with Andy Pafko. Playing for the Dodgers meant Jackie Robinson would be Uncle Rube's teammate for the next five years.

Uncle Rube had a nice, productive major league career, but will be forever known as the catcher who called the pitch in one of the most dramatic moments in baseball history, known as the "Shot Heard 'Round the World."

The October 3, 1951 playoff game between the Dodgers and the New York Giants remains a baseball classic.

In an era when baseball was far and away America's pastime, this game between two of baseball's most beloved teams encapsulated everything that was thrilling and frustrating and agonizing and wondrous about the sport.

The crosstown rivals had battled all season for National League supremacy. Just when it seemed the Dodgers would prevail; they began to falter as the season drew to a close. Meanwhile, the Giants won 37 of their final 44 games to tie the Dodgers for the regular season title.

A three-game playoff between the two teams followed with the Giants winning the first game and the Dodgers winning the second thanks to a home run by my uncle. That set the stage for the final game at the Polo Grounds.

It was also the first nationally televised baseball game in

history and was witnessed by millions of people, while millions more listened on the radio. The game was even broadcast on Armed Forces Radio to U.S. soldiers in some far-off land known as Korea.

My uncle had a prominent role in that game as the Dodgers' catcher. He was playing because starter, and future Hall of Famer, Roy Campanella was sidelined with an injury.

The Dodgers appeared to have the game in hand, leading 4-1 and seemingly on the way to meet the powerful and hated New York Yankees in the World Series.

Uncle Rube during his playing days. He was a catcher in the big leagues and is probably best known for being behind the plate for the Brooklyn Dodgers in 1951 when Bobby Thomson of the New York Giants hit the "Shot Heard Around the World" off Ralph Branca to clinch the National League pennant for the Giants. (Photo courtesy of Barney Sterling, Chicago Sports Photographer & Promotions)

Then the ninth inning happened.

After scoring one run to pull within 4-2 and with two Giants on base, the Dodgers' starting pitcher Don Newcombe was replaced by Ralph Branca to face the batter Bobby Thomson. With the count 1-0, my uncle called for Branca to throw a curveball to Thomson who promptly smacked it into the left field bleachers for the winning home run.

I've seen the video as Thomson runs into his entire team who was waiting for him at home plate to celebrate. My uncle can be seen slowing walking away toward the dugout, having no idea he and Thomson would be locked in baseball history together forever. There is even an exhibit of it at the Baseball Hall of Fame in Cooperstown, New York.

I do recall him being asked about Thomson's homerun when we were out somewhere. He just graciously smiled, looked down and shook his head saying, "I'd like to think he knew what pitch I called."

Part of the catcher's job is to know a hitter's weakness and call a pitch that the hitter can't hit. The catcher will flash signals to the pitcher telling him what pitch to throw. That's part of the wonderful non-verbal communication that makes baseball so special.

Then again, knowing what pitch is coming would give the hitter a small advantage in making the critical split-second swing adjustment that can mean the difference between success and failure.

In an attempt to defend his older brother, Uncle Leslie maintained that the Giants read the signal using a telescope placed strategically in Leo Durocher's office in the Giants' clubhouse.

I never heard Uncle Rube mention anything about a scandal. He always graciously smiled and shrugged it off. But rumors that the Giants had "stolen" signals raged for decades (and still do). In recent years, even Ralph Branca admitted that, just maybe, the Giants might have known what was coming – and this after years of never wanting to talk about it.

Ironically, Thomson and Branca actually became very good friends over the years, but the rumors have never really died away.

Just add that to the legend of one of baseball's most dramatic games.

This is how it went down according to a January 2001 article in the *Wall Street Journal* written by Joshua Harris Prager:

> The Giants had positioned a coach in the Giants' Clubhouse, specifically Leo Durocher's office, with a telescope to steal the signs of the catcher (Rube). Using some type of buzzer system, the coach with the telescope would tell the guys in the bullpen what pitch was about to be thrown and the bullpen guys would give a signal to the batter (Thomson).

Who knows for sure? In a strange twist of fate, my father would end up coaching with the ever-controversial Leo Durocher on the 1969 Cubs team, the same guy who was accused of stealing the signs from my uncle in 1951. My uncle's "Miracle Mets" pitching staff beat Durocher's Chicago Cubs that year in the epic Cubs Collapse of 1969. Maybe that made it even.

"What did my dad do?" I asked my mom, wondering how siblings would reconcile a National League Championship.

"When Rube beat Verlon in '69, he was so mad," Mom said. "Verlon came home to Lenoir and went fishing alone for three days."

Then she laughed.

It wasn't funny at the time. The typical older brother wins again.

"He was frustrated more than anything," Mom added.

That's all she would say. I wondered what the brothers said to each other after the World Series. I have always hoped to find a radio interview with them from that time. It seems that brothers who are coaches on opposing teams and battling each other to go to the World Series would be a novelty.

My uncle had great success with the New York Mets as pitching coach from 1968-1981. There he cultivated the talent of Nolan Ryan, Tom Seaver, Tug McGraw and Jerry Koosman – still considered one of the best pitching staffs in baseball history.

Uncle Rube also instituted "Walker's Law" which meant none of his pitchers threw a ball without him knowing about it. All of his pitchers were on fitness schedules that included running and strengthening the body. He focused on the mental aspects of the game instead of just the mechanics. Under his fatherly guidance, the pitchers thrived.

My cousin Barbie remembers, "Dad believed pitchers had to be very protective over their career. He would say, 'If you don't take care of yourself, who will?' He wanted each pitcher to have a long and productive career. They were more than an arm to my dad, he loved them.

"Dad would watch films of pitchers at home. He would examine them for hours. He would let us come in and actually discuss the mechanics of pitching. Dad would ask us questions and listen as we responded. We never gave a wrong answer but he made sure that we knew the better answer. I really did not think about it at the time, but Dad was sharing with us a wealth of knowledge of the game."

Along with Mets manager Gil Hodges, my uncle started the five-man rotation. Believing that an arm only had so many pitches in it, he extended the rest time from four to five days to keep the pitchers healthier over the course of a long baseball season.

Today a five-man rotation is commonplace in baseball, as franchises have realized just how valuable pitchers are and as the money invested in them demonstrates. But my uncle figured that out years ago.

The five-man rotation was never mentioned to me when I was a kid. It's a cool bit of trivia in hindsight, but not something my family discussed. There was never a conversation like, "Hey, did you know that Rube decided to use his pitchers every five days instead of every four days?" I did read that Tom Seaver was completely against it at first.

My uncle completed his career as the pitching coach for the Atlanta Braves alongside manager Joe Torre.

In 1992, Joe Torre came to Rube's funeral in Lenoir. This was before he went on to his successful stint as manager of the New York Yankees, where he won four World Series titles in five years. I did not know who he was. So, in 1996 when the Atlanta Braves played the Yankees in the World Series and as the teams were being announced, I saw Torre and thought to myself, "Hey, that guy was at my uncle's funeral a few years ago."

My mom likes to tell the story about coming in second in a golf tournament at Lenoir Golf Course with Rube as her partner.

Rube drew her name to be his partner for the tournament and while my mom was a decent golfer, Rube was definitely the stronger of the two. He loved the competition but never let it exceed the fun. My mom jokes she couldn't have won with my dad.

One story that haunted my uncle for years was the death of his friend and Mets manager Gil Hodges, one of the great underappreciated baseball minds in history.

On the afternoon of April 2, 1972, Hodges was in West Palm Beach, Florida, completing a round of golf with Mets coaches Joe Pignatano, Eddie Yost and my uncle. Hodges collapsed on his way to the team motel and Pignatano later recalled Hodges falling backwards and hitting his head on the sidewalk with a "sickening knock."

He was bleeding profusely and turning blue and Pignatano said, "I put my hand under Gil's head, but before you knew it, the blood stopped. I knew he was dead. He died in my arms."

A lifelong chain smoker, Hodges had suffered a heart attack and was dead almost before he hit the ground. He died just two days before his 48th birthday.

Uncle Rube retired in 1984. He would always be attached to the old Brooklyn Dodgers. In 2004, a former teammate, Carl Erskine, wrote a book "Carl Erskine's Tales from the Dodgers' Dugout: Extra Innings." My uncle found his way into a number of Erskine's stories.

Uncle Rube was never a great major league ballplayer. He'd be the first to admit that. But he played 11 seasons with the Chicago Cubs and with the Dodgers, both in Brooklyn and Los Angeles. He was a career .227 hitter and hit 35 home runs in 608 games. There are many players who would have loved that kind of career.

Uncle Rube died of lung cancer on December 14, 1992. He was just 66 years old. He is buried in his beloved Lenoir, just like his brothers.

Dan Rather, the former news anchor for *CBS Evening News,* wrote the following article about Uncle Rube which was published in *The Nation* on July 27, 2011.

Rube Walker

Third-string catchers are rarely anybody's hero, but Rube Walker was and remains one of mine. I met him when he was headed down and out of the major leagues. He'd been a player with the Cubs and Dodgers—only a .227 lifetime hitter, but the classic "rocking chair" catcher whom pitchers love. With his ever-present chaw of tobacco and a drawl as Southern as frost on cotton leaves, he was a throwback to the rural poverty of America in the first half of the twentieth century. In 1959, he'd just become a player-manager with the Triple-A Houston Buffaloes. I was a full-time general reporter moonlighting as the radio play-by-play man for the Buffs.

Rube took me and my wife, Jean, newlyweds all young, fresh, eager and ambitious, under his wing—treated us like a father. He had a heart as big as a locomotive, full of compassion, generosity and understanding. He helped the community's poor; he taught young players and counseled old ones; he was a jovial encourager to everyone. In so doing, he taught us what it was to be a "big leaguer," in the best, most noble sense of the term.

The Buffs fired him in midseason, on Father's Day. When he told us, tears welled in Jean's eyes. Rube touched her on the shoulder and said, "Don't fret, hon'. Life's full of curveballs."

It's true. Life is full of curveballs. Even when you are expecting one, it can be a bit of a shock. The audacity of contrast stops us cold.

It occurs to me now that I never had the courage to ask my Uncle Rube some basic questions about my dad. I had learned that it was best to just pretend I had adjusted to the death of my father. The truth was, my father's death was an unexpected curveball. It froze all of us at the plate including my uncle, a seasoned veteran adept at spotting them. None of us knew what to say or do and nobody knew exactly what to do about me. I relieved them of their burden by bluffing that I was fine.

But I would have wanted to know how my father felt about me. I would have wanted to know what he taught me and what his hopes and dreams were for me. I'd want to know what he would have wanted my life to be like and what he would have said to me in times of trouble.

Would it have made any difference hearing such things from my uncle? Would he have even known? I don't know.

But I think if I had asked, Uncle Rube would have smiled at me and told me everything I wanted and needed to hear. He would have said my dad's world was my mom and me and everything Dad did, everything he was, revolved around us.

And I would have believed it, especially after I came to learn about who my dad really was.

Would it have been true?

> *Dear Dad,*
>
> *You, Rube and Leslie believed in family above all else. You took care of your parents and each other. You left legacies of love behind.*
>
> *Your brothers tried to fill in for you in my life, especially Uncle Leslie.*
>
> *If ya'll are together right now, you are drinking Early Times bourbon, Uncle Les is smoking a cigarette and Uncle Rube is swinging a golf club.*
>
> *The topic of conversation is the Cubs winning the World Series in 2016.*
>
> *LA*
>
> *PS- How did you really feel when Uncle Rube's Mets beat your Cubs in 1969? That was a total curveball.*

CHAPTER 4
A Real Love Story

After my father died, Mom and I left Chicago to my parents' hometown of Lenoir to live with her mother, Minnie Wilson, in a large white house on several acres of land. John Wilson, Mom's brother, lived close by and was a positive and happy role model for me. Mom created a comfortable life for us while making her transition from wife to widow.

We didn't discuss my dad.

One summer Sunday afternoon I was sitting on the front porch swing with my grandmother. I was six years old. She was a brawny, no-nonsense woman. I saw her cry one time, right before she died because she was in physical pain, nothing emotional.

Always busy in the garden or kitchen, she sang from the Baptist hymn book, and not very well. She knew every word and to be honest, those words scared me a little. One of her favorite hymns was "Blessed Assurance" which talks about being washed in blood. I know it was supposed to be a symbolic image, but I took it literally because that's what kids do. Washed in blood? That would just make a mess.

On this particular day, my grandmother was methodically

stringing beans and pushing the swing back and forth with her legs. Her hands and feet were connected in a sort of stringing, swinging motion. I liked being there beside her.

We had just been to church which was supposed to make me feel better but it didn't. I wanted to believe in God. I wanted to feel what it seemed like others were feeling, but I just couldn't. Everyone had caught the Holy Spirit but me. I played along, mimicking what I saw but I felt nothing.

On that swing, I broke my silence and told my grandmother, "I want my dad." She stopped stringing, stood up, looked down at me and said, "I know you miss him. We all miss him. If your mama hears you say that, it will upset her. I don't want you to say that ever again. You hear me?"

She touched my shoulder gently and said, "It was God's will." Then she walked into the house carrying her pot of strung beans. The door shut behind her. I sat there swinging, staring at a pile of bean strings on the ground. Alone.

I never talked about it again.

My grandmother was protecting her daughter. In her own strong way she was saying to me, "Let's not state the obvious. There is nothing we can do about it. God meant for it to happen." What I learned that day was that if I talk about my dad, it upsets the people I love.

She missed him. My mom missed him. Leo Durocher might have missed him but I didn't even know him. I had this giant empty hole inside me with no idea what could fill it.

From that exchange, I made the conscious decision not to discuss my feelings, particularly if it made others uncomfortable, no matter what it cost me. I pretended to be just fine even when I wasn't. Furthermore, if God did this, he was cruel and probably did wash people in blood.

Dear Anger,
Hello my fiery friend.
I feel you like electricity all over my body.
Fearless, puffed up, certain
Thank goodness you came.
On my downhill slide into depression you grabbed me by
*   the throat and slung me into this moment.*
I landed on my feet, battle ready.
My teeth grit together and my jaw flexes
Who is my foe, though?
God?
LA

Mom would occasionally tell me a story about Dad that always ended with, "and you were the apple of his eye." I never brought him up or asked questions. We were both suspended in this grief together and equally reluctant to discuss it.

When I decided to begin this quest, I did not start by talking with her. Instead, I told her about my plans and kept her posted about who I talked to. I would rummage through boxes of pictures asking her, "Who is this?" She would put on her glasses, look closely and she'd either identify the person or look puzzled. I was, after all, asking her to remember faces from 50 years ago.

Once I had some success contacting people and learning about Dad, I realized it was time for me to sit down with my mom.

One weekend, I left my kids with my husband and I went to see her. My stepfather had recently died and for the first time in many years it was just me and her. I was at a good place emotionally, feeling confident, elated even, about all I had heard about my dad.

I wanted to hear about their love story.

"How did you meet Dad?" I asked.

She took a deep breath, "His cousin Hildred Clark told him to ask me out. Verlon called me on Tuesday to ask me to the football game on Friday night."

"Did you say yes?" I asked, smiling.

"No, I told him I'd think about it," she laughed.

"Why? What did you have to think about?"

"I don't know…that's just the way we did it back then. I called him the next day and said I would go."

They went on their first date to a Lenoir High School football game in October of 1957, but didn't marry until 1966. It was a nine-year courtship which was pretty radical for the time.

"Why did you wait so long to get married?"

"He didn't ask me," she replied, almost sassy.

"Were you discouraged? You wanted to marry him, right?" I pushed.

"Oh, I wanted to marry him but he was traveling so much with baseball and he thought it was no kind of life for me. I was working at the bank in Lenoir. I liked my job." She said it in a matter of fact tone.

I felt like she was hiding a multitude of love and passion behind facts.

I asked her to tell me about a time when she visited him while they were dating.

"I'll try. That was a long time ago."

She paused.

"Maybe I'll dream about it tonight," she replied.

"Maybe you will. I love you, mama," I said.

I love you, too," she reached out and hugged me.

I was forcing her to make an uncomfortable and probably unexpected trip back in time. It hadn't occurred to me that she might be protecting her heart just like I used to protect mine when people asked about my dad.

Mom was a stunning beauty with big hazel eyes and full exotic lips. An elegant slim figure masked a bit of the clumsy. She was an independent thinker refusing to settle into the traditional role as wife and mother, reliant on a man.

Her father owned a grocery store. He had told her, "Annie, go into banking. It's a stable job that pays well." She went to work at a bank in Lenoir, bought her own car and eventually bought her own home. One by one, her friends got married. She was a bridesmaid at every one of them. By age 28, she was in danger of being branded an "old maid."

That's when she met my dad.

It was October 1957. He was home for the winter from his minor-league stint in Paris, Illinois, where he was the player/manager. It had been a good baseball season for him as a player. He batted .321 and hit 20 home runs. His brother Rube was the famous hometown boy playing for the Brooklyn Dodgers.

Mom was not impressed with the fact that he was a baseball player with a famous brother. When he called to ask her out, she couldn't quite place who he was. They had gone to different schools. He had left 10 years earlier, returning only for short periods of time and he usually spent that time hunting and fishing. Their paths didn't cross.

When I was back home, I called Mom a few days later to see if she had dreamed of any stories from their courtship. I had always been uncomfortable discussing him with Mom. I didn't even know whether to refer to him as "my dad" or "Verlon" when talking to her.

She told me about visiting him when he played in Paris, Illinois and Carlsbad, New Mexico before they married. I was getting a snapshot of his baseball life. Even when he was with the Cubs, the hotels weren't grand, transportation was mediocre and the pay was pennies compared to today.

My dad always made local friends wherever he played. They were baseball fans, business owners, kids. They all knew him and would embrace my mom when she visited. In Paris, a local man who had an airplane took mom flying several times.

"It was a small plane, room for one passenger. I had never been in a small plane before," Mom recalled.

"Were you afraid?" I asked.

"Not at first," she laughed, "I got in my seat and there was a picture of Jesus in the cockpit in front of me. The man pointed at the picture and said, 'Jesus is my co-pilot.'"

"Did that put you at ease?" I asked.

"Yeah, until I went back to Paris the next year and found out that man had died in a plane crash." Mom and I laughed. I guess it really wasn't funny but, well....

One afternoon, I found a large trunk under the bed at my mom's house. I don't remember ever seeing it before. When I pulled it out, there were Cubs stickers all over it.

I unlocked the double-hinged safety hasps and opened it. The smell of old paper and moth balls floated past me. Like buried treasure, I unpacked layers and layers of stuff, displaying it on the floor in front of me.

A stack of letters, rubber-banded together, caught my attention. Letters addressed to my mom with *Verlon Walker* as the sender. My heart began to race. Letters from my dad to my mom!

I opened each one carefully examining his handwriting. I paused on every word like I was drinking it in with my eyes. I was intruding on their love story but I couldn't help myself.

Dad wrote to her for nine years and he sent her newspaper clippings of every game. She made elaborate scrap books with the newspaper articles. It was all hidden away in a steamer trunk under a bed. How had I never seen this before?

It was insight into his dry humor, kindness, and deep love

for my mother in black and white. I enjoyed those more than the tape of his voice. It was authentic affection. The way he talked to her in the letters made me sad. She must have missed him terribly when he died. It was heartbreaking to be loved like that and have it taken away.

What struck me was his balance between wanting her to be his, yet understanding that it wasn't fair to ask her to put her life on hold while he played baseball. He encouraged her to have her own life. His love for her was rich with respect.

I also saw him use his sense of humor to display vulnerability. I do that, too.

"Have you been out on any dates? I haven't. I'm surrounded by mean, ugly women here," he wrote in one of the letters.

He complimented her often. "If you were here in Paris, Illinois," he wrote, "you would cause a stir all over town. They haven't seen pretty like you."

I loved the way he talked to her. It made me think about the way he would have talked to me and the way I wanted to be loved.

In truth, Verlon was not looking for a love. There was no room for a relationship in his minor-league life, but my mom proved to be different. He hadn't expected someone like her. She allowed him the space to chase his baseball dream and he didn't demand that she be a traditional woman and give up her job to be with him. They were comfortable in the knowledge that they had carved out lives that made them happy. Together, they made it work.

The next time Mom and I got together, I asked her about that force of nature known as Leo Durocher.

"He was unpredictable," she said. "You just never knew what he was going to do. But he trusted your dad."

Leo Durocher certainly belongs in baseball's lengthy pantheon of interesting characters. Brilliant, frustrating, infuriating,

Durocher joins the likes of guys like Babe Ruth, Casey Stengel, Ty Cobb, Reggie Jackson, Billy Martin and others who made the game special in ways that are still being dissected.

It's necessary here to give just a little background on this guy who was known as "Leo the Lip." And anyone who knew Durocher knew that nickname was well earned.

He played for four different Major League teams – the New York Yankees, Cincinnati Reds, St. Louis Cardinals and Brooklyn Dodgers – and while he was considered a pretty slick infielder, he wasn't much of a hitter. In fact, Babe Ruth would often tease him by calling him the "All-American Out."

But Yankees manager Miller Huggins saw in Durocher a scrappy, competitive, smart guy who he thought might have the makings of a pretty good manager one day.

He got his first opportunity to manage the Dodgers in 1939 and would go on to manage three other teams: the New York Giants, the Cubs and Houston Astros over the course of the next three decades. Durocher returned to managing after years away in the broadcast booth and famously put an end to the Cubs' "College of Coaches" by simply saying at his introductory press conference that "I'm not a head coach, I'm the manager."

His stint with the Cubs would run from 1966 to 1972. In that time, he led a team that would bounce from one end of the spectrum to the other. His first season in Chicago in 1966, the Cubs were simply awful, winning just 59 games. In the years to follow, the Cubs were actually quite competitive, averaging more than 80 wins a season.

Durocher's career with the Cubs, of course, included the infamous 1969 season when he led his team to a seemingly insurmountable nine-game division lead in mid-August. But the New York Mets, forever known as the "Amazin' Mets" began their surge and the Cubs collapsed.

It was that 1969 season when the Walker brothers would meet in the National League Division Series as coaches for opposing teams – my dad with the Cubs and my uncle with the Mets. They had come a long way from hitting golf balls wrapped in yarn in vacant fields with a cereal box as home plate in Lenoir, North Carolina.

Durocher remained manager until he was forced out in the middle of the 1972 season. He then took over as manager of the Astros and retired after the 1973 season. He won 2,009 games as a manager and is in the Hall of Fame for his accomplishments.

"Did Leo Durocher trust my dad to make baseball decisions?" I asked my mom.

"Verlon smoothed things over for Leo in the clubhouse," she said. "He just trusted your dad to talk to the players, to the

This is my favorite picture of my parents taken at a party at Cedar Rock Country Club September 1959, just two years into their courtship. A moment in time that captured their love. (Photo Courtesy of Ward Story)

front office. He knew your dad would make things right. Get things done, you know," Mom explained.

She recalled a story when Durocher was divorced from actress Laraine Day but still had a house near hers in Hollywood, California. He wanted one of his cars taken to the house and asked my dad to drive it there. Mom said my dad came home proclaiming, "We're going to Hollywood!" Dad drove Leo's car as mom followed in their car from Chicago to Los Angeles.

"What did the house look like?" I asked.

"It was just a house on the side of a hill," Mom laughed.

It was an adventure for them, from small-town Lenoir to Hollywood.

The only time my mom saw my dad angry at Leo was when Durocher ran off during the 1969 All-Star break to marry his fourth wife, Lynne Goldblatt.

"Verlon thought he could have waited," Mom said.

Leo Durocher was quite famous and being out with him was always an experience. One evening all the coaches went to dinner at one of those fancy Chicago night clubs. In walks the infamous Rat Pack – Dean Martin, Frank Sinatra and Sammy Davis, Jr. Leo invited them to the table.

"I couldn't believe it," Mom said. "The Rat Pack at our table!"

"Did they talk to you?" I asked.

"I was too shy to say anything," she replied. "I just smiled a lot."

"I would have been star-struck," I offered.

"Leo had made fun of my Southern accent," she said. "I was self-conscious, but your dad laughed and joked with them. That's the way he was."

Leo respected that my dad was comfortable with who he was, that he worked hard and knew baseball. When my dad got sick in 1971, Leo visited the hospital many times.

"I was practically living at the hospital," Mom said. "I didn't want to leave your dad. You were staying with the players and coaches' families. Late one afternoon, Leo walked in. He brought me a book and sat with us for a long time. I think he really was sad."

My parents had to love each other like crazy in order to sustain a nine-year courtship on only their terms. In the end, and against all the odds, it made for the ideal relationship. Love stories, the truly great ones, have something unique.

"What do you have planned for Saturday?" Verlon asked.

"I might go to the mountains," Mom replied. "Why?"

"Let's get married," he said with a smile.

On a Saturday in February 1966, they married in Gaffney, South Carolina with only their parents attending. They went to South Carolina because there was no waiting period for a marriage license there. Verlon Walker didn't want to spend another baseball season apart. The following Saturday, Mr. and Mrs. Verlon Walker left for spring training together.

Dad was diagnosed with leukemia a year later. I was born two years later. They packed as much life as they could in five years. We lived in a small apartment in Lincoln Park in Chicago. These were some of the happiest years of my mother's life.

My father became sick during spring training February 1971. His leukemia which had gone into remission was back. Mom relied on the coaches and player's wives to take care of me while she stayed with him at the hospital. I was passed around from Bob Kennedy to Joe Becker to Ernie Banks. I was passed around for two weeks while she sat beside him in the hospital.

She dropped me off with Ernie Banks one evening thinking that I would enjoy playing with his daughter. Within an hour, I was inconsolable to the point that Ernie actually went to the pharmacy to ask if there was anything he could give me to calm me down. Think of it: "Mr. Cub" on the hunt for something to stop my crying.

I couldn't wrap my two-year-old brain around what was happening. I would conclude that people disappear. They go away and don't come back. The worst does happen. My father had "unfinished business" with me.

I decided I would ask Mom to tell me about the day my father died. This was a subject we both were adept at avoiding. I was uncomfortable about bringing him up. I called her almost every morning just to check in. She's 87 after all.

"Good morning, Mama! How did you sleep last night?"

"I haven't had my coffee yet," she replied.

I went straight for it.

"Mom, I want to ask you some questions about the day my dad died."

"Is this for the book?" she asked.

"It's for me, but it might make the book," I said. I didn't want her to hold back on what she said.

"Well....I haven't forgotten Verlon. I still think of him every day, but the details are foggy," she said.

I never thought she forgot him. I believed she couldn't handle remembering him. After a short pause, she began talking in a stream of consciousness manner as if she were piecing the memories together as she went.

"They removed his spleen in Arizona during spring training in February. I think that's right," Mom paused. "I can't remember the sequence, but we ended up back in Chicago in the hospital. I don't remember how I got back to Chicago," she said, struggling to place it correctly in her mind.

"Did he know he was dying?" I asked nervously.

Her voice was breathy and a bit shaky. She would start and stop, and start again.

"Uncle Leslie picked you up at the airport in Charlotte. I got on the next plane back to Chicago," she continued. "Then Rube picked

A Real Love Story

you and mother up in Lenoir, and drove to Chicago a week later."

"So, you flew with me to Charlotte, handed me to Uncle Les and got on a plane back to Chicago?" I asked in clarification.

"Yes. I didn't want to be away from Verlon and I couldn't take care of you," she responded.

I resolved to let her talk. I would let her tell me what she could without interruptions and questions. She hadn't answered my question about if he knew he was dying. I was going to leave it there and wait.

Mom continued to tell me about his last day as if it came from deep inside her, fighting its way out to me. Taking detours, she talked about clothing that was worn, a meal she had at a nearby restaurant, and visiting hours at the hospital.

"Verlon was weak. But when Rube brought you to the hospital, he lit up."

I could hear a smile come over her.

"You have his personality, you know" she said. "He would be proud of you."

She told me I sat on his chest that was sick with pneumonia and clapped my hands. I was 2 1/2. That's where he left me.

"His last thoughts were of you that day. He knew he was dying," Mom said. "Rube took you back to the apartment while I sat beside Verlon on his bed. He gave me instructions about what he wanted for you. I cried while he talked."

Mom took a deep breath.

"I told him, she's going to be all I've got, so I'll do my best," Mom began to cry.

"You have been an amazing mama," I reassured her. "I'm a good mom because you were. I love you, my children love you."

Just like that, all the awkwardness and tension of the moment melted away. We were both with him in our minds and it was peaceful.

93

"A few hours later, he just quit breathing. He had the sweetest smile on his face when he passed," Mom's voice quivered a little. We sat quiet for a few seconds. I was grateful I had finally asked and relieved that she had shared. I was in awe of her strength.

He died March 24, 1971, in Wesley Memorial Hospital in Chicago with my mother by his side. Her happily-ever-after love story was over. They were both 42.

Dear Dad,

I want to tell you about mom.

Against her better judgment, she bought me an expensive magenta, sequin prom dress with closed toe satin high heels dyed to match because that is what I wanted.

She was holding her newborn grandson the morning of September 11 2001. I had just gotten home from the hospital. I was a terrified new mother afraid of my baby and the changing world. She saved me.

After you died, she bought a house in a neighborhood in Lenoir that had a bunch of kids so I would make friends.

I went to college, left college, went back to college, graduated from college, went back to college for another degree. She paid for it all.

At 87, she is sassy, funny and active. Driving herself around and talking on a cell phone but not at the same time. She takes exercise and computer classes. She plays cards every Friday night with her girlfriends.

She's been worried about me lately.

She did everything you asked her to do and more and she never got over you.

You were the love of her life.

LA

CHAPTER 5
Putting the Pieces Together

I confess. I was hooked on researching him.

I looked for connections and continued to contact people. I would say, "Tell me anything you remember about my dad. If you know that he liked sunflower seeds, tell me. I don't know that stuff. There is no detail too small."

I was trusting the metaphorical current again to guide me. My anger had gone dormant for the moment. I had relaxed a bit in the unfamiliar water. The more I relaxed, the more I received. It was almost intoxicating to find out something new about him. I spent my extra time secretly researching baseball, baseball in the 1960s, and anyone who might have known my dad.

I tracked down a baseball historian in Eastern North Carolina, Marty Tschetter, who contacted the Baseball Hall of Fame on my behalf to inquire about archives. Cooperstown did a search which unfortunately did not turn up any radio or TV archives of my dad.

I contacted Ron Barber, a baseball collector, who compiled every known clip of Jack Quinlan and his partner Lou Boudreau, WGN announcers, in an audio CD called *Quinlan – Forgotten Greatness*. Ron encouraged my journey and even reached out to Bob Costas for me.

Bob Costas said he knew my uncle and suggested I contact the Mets organization to see if they had any interview archives that might include my uncle and father since they were on opposing teams during the 1969 National League Division Series. I did, and they didn't.

I enjoyed the pursuit of Dad even when I found nothing. I couldn't believe how eager people were to help me.

Charles Shriver was the Cubs public relations director in the 1960s. I can't remember who gave me his phone number but I left him a long message explaining who I was. Chuck called me one afternoon while I was driving home from the grocery store. I pulled over and scribbled these notes on a paper bag.

"All the players liked your dad," Chuck said. "They went to him with problems. He was good listener. People just enjoyed being around him."

I took a breath and said, "I've heard a lot about his humor."

"He was really quick-witted," Chuck said. "He kept everyone laughing."

He related a story from a long-ago spring training.

"A bunch of the guys were walking back to the hotel from dinner and were approached by a prostitute. And she says, 'Any of you wanna have a good time?' So, Rube looks at me and says, 'Brush that hayseed off my shoulder, will ya?'"

He laughed at my dad referring to his Lenoir, North Carolina upbringing. Basically, my dad was saying, "She must think I'm a fool, a country bumpkin, a 'rube.'" His humor was many times self-deprecating. He was making others comfortable by making fun of himself. One must be confident to pull that off. My dad had country confidence.

Chuck continued, "In baseball, there is a lot of downtime. Your dad was just fun to be around, easy going. He made the downtime fun."

A photo of myself, Mom and Dad when he was a coach for the Chicago Cubs. I don't have many examples of family photos and each one I have is special. This one was taken in 1969. It has been hard to talk with mom about my dad because I know it still hurts for her even though it's been more than 40 years since he died. But she opened up to me as I wrote this book and I appreciate that because I know it wasn't easy. (Photo courtesy of Barney Sterling, Chicago Sports Photographer & Promotions)

Dad stands with another of the great players of the 1960s, Cincinnati Reds' outfielder Frank Robinson. Robinson had 10 great seasons with the Reds from 1956-65 before being traded to the Baltimore Orioles where he continued to be one of baseball's top players and eventual Hall of Famer. (Photo courtesy of Barney Sterling, Chicago Sports Photographer & Promotions)

Here's my dad at one his stops in minor league baseball. My dad was never a great player but he was good enough to spend a few years in the Cubs organization first as a player then as a coach in places like Lumberton, North Carolina; San Antonio, Texas; Wenatchee, Washington and Paris, Illinois. Eventually, he got his shot to coach in the major leagues with the Chicago Cubs and he could not have been happier.

My dad poses with one of his favorite people in baseball, New York Mets manager, Casey Stengel. Stengel hired my Uncle Rube as his pitching coach. The Mets and Cubs had an epic battle for the National League East title in 1969 but my dad's Cubs lost out. (Photo courtesy of Al Walker)

I fulfilled a long-time dream by visiting Wrigley Field in 2015. When the Cubs organization heard what I was doing, they were so helpful giving me access to the people and places I wanted to see. The people currently at the Chicago Cubs' front office may not have known my dad, but they knew the stories of his kindness and generosity. Here, I'm sitting in the dugout by myself. I like to think I'm in the exact same spot as Dad and I sat to have our picture taken over 34 years ago – the photo used on this book's cover. (Photo courtesy of Johnny Burbano Photography)

The two most important people in my life are my sons: Walker, left, and Christopher. They are aware of my journey to learn about Dad. I'm trying to let them know just how respected their grandfather was for his kindness and calm demeanor. If he were still alive, he would want to teach them how important it is to be kind and respectful. And, probably how to throw a curve ball.

Here is my dad in the dugout with legendary Pittsburgh Pirates radio announcer Bob (The Gunner) Prince. Bob was famed for his loud sport coats, as you can tell. In the middle is famed former Brooklyn Dodgers shortstop Pee Wee Reese, who until 1964 teamed with Dizzy Dean on CBS' Game of the Week. It aired in Charlotte (Channel 3), but not in any big-league markets like Chicago. (Photo courtesy of Barney Sterling, Chicago Sports Photographer & Promotions)

One of my favorite photos of me with Uncle Rube when he was a pitching coach with the New York Mets. As I got older, we would talk a little about my dad, but the conversations often ended quickly, No one really wanted to talk about it. (Photo courtesy of Ann Walker)

100

My dad got along with everybody, even the umpires. In this photo where everyone seems to be having a good time, my dad is on the far right, from left Cubs pitcher Larry Jackson, long-time National League umpire and Chicago native Jocko Conlan, and third baseman Ron Santo. (Photo courtesy of Barney Sterling, Chicago Sports Photographer & Promotions)

I seemed to make the rounds with a lot of the New York Mets coaches when I was a little girl. In this photo, another of my favorites, I'm being held by the great New York Yankees catcher Yogi Berra, who at the time was a coach for the New York Mets with my Uncle Rube. (Photo courtesy of Barney Sterling, Chicago Sports Photographer & Promotions)

Another picture of me with Uncle Rube during his days with the New York Mets. My dad and he looked a lot alike, didn't they? And though Uncle Rube had a more successful Major League career than my dad, Dad did not have any bitterness or jealousy to get in the way of respecting and loving his older brother – although there were some frustrating times during the 1969 Mets and Cubs series! (Photo courtesy of Ann Walker)

This is me, all by myself this time, on a walkway at Wrigley Field. I certainly didn't understand what Dad did for a living when I was a little girl and it wasn't much clearer as I got older. I just knew he was involved in baseball and a lot of people knew him. I didn't know how much he was respected until I began this journey of discovery. (Photo courtesy of Ann Walker)

A wedding photo of Mom and Dad taken in February 1966. They had known each other in Lenoir for years and began a sweet and often long-distance courtship that would last nine years until they were finally married. No happy ending to this fairy tale romance, as my dad died five years later. (Photo Courtesy of John Wilson, Ann Walker's brother)

This is the first photo where I could really see my dad's piercing and kind blue eyes. It is the image I have always kept of him. I gave this photo a prominent spot next to my bed as I watched the Cubs beat the Cleveland Indians in the 2016 World Series. I'm convinced my dad's spirit helped the Cubs rally for the championship. (Photo courtesy of Barney Sterling, Chicago Sports Photographer & Promotions)

I suppose this was one of my dad's duties as a coach for the Cubs. He's posing with Cubs third baseman Ron Santo and Evelyn LaHaie, the Chicago area "Miss Physical Fitness" as part of a local marketing campaign. Interesting trivia: LaHaie became an actress and talent scout and was, apparently, the person who suggested that a little-known musical group from Gary, Indiana change its name to the "Jackson 5." I think that worked out. (Photo courtesy of Barney Sterling, Chicago Sports Photographer & Promotions)

My dad congratulates Ernie Banks after hitting a two-run homer in a 1964 game against the St. Louis Cardinals. Dad did this more than a few times in his years as the Cubs' third base coach. Banks hit 512 home runs in this 19-year career with the Cubs that ended in 1971 – the same year my dad died. 512 home runs is still second-best in team history behind Sammy Sosa. (Photo courtesy of United Press International)

My dad standing with his favorite bourbon in his hand with some of the 1969 Cubs coaches and players gathered around. From left, Dad, Pete Reiser, Joe Becker. and Joey Amalfitano. They may be celebrating a victory, but we won't know. Remember? What happens in the clubhouse, stays in the clubhouse. (Photo courtesy of Barney Sterling, Chicago Sports Photographer & Promotions)

The four coaches for the Chicago Cubs in 1966 were from right, manager Leo Durocher, Freddie Fitzsimmons, my father and first base coach, Whitey Lockman. It was, to be charitable, not a good season for the Cubs who staggered in with a club-worst 103 losses. Ironically, Lockman took over for Durocher in 1972 as the Cubs manager and lasted through the 1974 season. (Photo courtesy of Barney Sterling, Chicago Sports Photographer & Promotions)

1956 DES MOINES BRUINS

Standing, Left to Right—Trainer Ben Mankowski, Hal Meek, Marty Garber, George Piktuzis, Paul Hoffmeister, Jerry Sheehan, John Andre, Russ Wingo, Ernie Johnson, Gene Steiger, Buzz Clarkson, Don Swanson, and Manager Lou Klein
Sitting, Left to Right—Eddie Haas, Bob McKee, Jim Stoddard, Tom Legros, Rube Walker, John Reider, Ted Sterger, Tom Nerad, John Hricinak, and Bud McClure.
Batboys, Left to Right—Terry Lipovac and Charlie Savich.

Another team photo from another minor league team my dad played on over the years. This is the 1956 Des Moines, Iowa Bruins, a Class A team in the Western League that was an affiliate of the Chicago Cubs. That's my dad, fifth from the left sitting down, looking pretty serious. (Photo courtesy of Ken Scarpino)

This is a favorite photo of my dad. He would always tell Cubs' players and coaches that coming to the ballpark every day made him smile. (Photo courtesy of Ann Walker)

My mom and I having some quiet time together. I didn't realize until years later just how difficult my dad's death was on her and how she suffered in relative silence. It has only been recently that she has opened up and shared with about dad's death in 1971 leaving a hole in her life. (Photo courtesy of Ann Walker)

Happy smiles for my dad and me – and he's not wearing a baseball uniform! I miss him every day but being able to speak with people who knew him has helped me work through the grief and come out the other side, hopefully, a better person. (Photo courtesy of Ann Walker)

The bronze plaque is on the brick sign in front of Walker Stadium in Lenoir. I don't know where that phrase came from but I love it and it has sustained me over the years and I am grateful for that.

My dad is standing on the far right of this team photo of the 1957 Paris, Illinois Lakers of the Class D Midwest League, the low minor league affiliate of the Cubs. My dad played in small towns all over the country. In Paris, he was a player/coach which was a job he loved. In fact, he had his best season as a pro in Paris, hitting .321 with 20 home runs. (Photo courtesy Benjamin Studio, Paris, Illinois)

Members of the Chicago Cubs experimental and ultimately ill-fated "College of Coaches" gather prior to the 1961 season. Standing: Rip Collins, Goldie Holt, My dad, and Charlie Grimm. Seated are El Tappe, Harry Craft, team owner William Wrigley and Vedie Himsl. The College of Coaches was created to give each coach a chance to alternate as manager while the others served as various coaches. It was, simply, a disaster. The first year in 1961, the Cubs lost 90 games and the next season they lost 103. And while they did improve their record, by 1965, the college was falling apart and Leo Durocher came in as the one and only manager in 1966. He retained my dad as the bullpen coach even though, at first, he didn't want to. (Photo Courtesy Chicago Sun-Times)

This was a special photo for my dad as he stands with the great Los Angeles Dodgers pitcher Sandy Koufax. This photo was taken probably in 1967 or 1968 when Koufax had quit baseball at the height of his career in 1966 (at age 31) and signed on to do color commentary for NBC-TV. (Photo courtesy of Barney Sterling, Chicago Sports Photographer & Promotions)

This is a photo clipping from the April 6, 1971 Chicago Tribune. That was a difficult day for everyone, including me. The Cubs and St. Louis Cardinals held a moment silence in honor of my dad at Wrigley Field. His death impacted many players on the team as well as players around the league. I didn't know until years later just what an impact he had on people.

This is a neat photo from 1980 as Cubs' radio announcer Milo Hamilton interviews Cubs' pitcher Bruce Sutter, who is wearing a special RUBE jacket in honor of my dad. Sutter is promoting a fundraiser in honor of the Rube Walker Blood Center and in the middle is Dr. Wilson Hartz, the director of the center. (Photo courtesy of Barney Sterling, Chicago Sports Photographer & Promotions)

A candid shot of three Chicago Cubs' coaches, from left, Joe Becker, Leo Durocher and my dad. It was taken mid-season on July 8, 1970. I learned that Leo was a "tough boss" with his coaches and the team. Leo respected my dad's opinion and calm demeanor. (Photo Courtesy of Barney Sterling, Chicago Sports Photographer & Promotions)

I owe a huge debt of thanks to Pat Hughes, the Cubs play-by-play radio announcer, who helped my journey get off the ground by simply listening to my story and giving me a place to start. Even though he didn't know who I was when I contacted him, he helped me in ways I will never forget. When I visited Chicago in the summer of 2015 I went to the press box at Wrigley Field and finally got a chance to meet Pat and say thank you. (Photo courtesy Johnny Burbano Photography)

What a great honor. On May 20, 2017, I was asked to throw out the first pitch of the season for the Lenoir Oilers of the Carolina-Virginia Collegiate League. It was a beautiful day and as I stood on the field at Walker Stadium, named after my dad and my uncle, I couldn't help but think both were watching. Unfortunately, my pitch didn't quite reach the plate and I wondered if I'd had my dad to teach me, I might have done a better job. Still, it was an experience I will never forget and I am so thankful that General Manager Kevin Bumgarner asked me to do it. (Photo courtesy of David Laxton)

I wanted Mom with me on this first game of the 2017 season for the Lenoir Oilers. She has been through a lot over the years as she tried to deal with the death of her first real love and she has done it with grace and fortitude. She told more stories about my dad in recent years as I worked through my feelings, but I think she has kept some memories just for herself. And maybe that's the way it should be. (Photo courtesy of David Laxton)

Chuck Shriver is friends with Mary Deese and wrote to her on my behalf. Mary was the executive secretary for John Holland, the Chicago Cubs general manager in the 1960s. Chuck thought she might have a story about my dad.

Mary Deese was the first woman I contacted on my journey. Right from the beginning, I loved her. She rushed forth with a happy energy and a soft voice. I needed her. I just didn't know how much. She spoke to me in a different way than the men. She spoke in a delicate, playful, ladylike way that, frankly, I had been missing as I went along on this journey.

"Hey Hon! How are you today?" Mary's greeting practically overwhelmed me.

"Mary, tell me everything you know about my dad," I said, as if I was talking to an old friend.

My dad, far left, celebrates a victory with two of his favorite players, Don Kessinger and Ernie Banks. It seems every player I talked to respected and genuinely liked my dad. His quick wit and easy manner made him a favorite, especially to young players trying to earn their way onto the team. They called him a "good" man, and that meant a lot to me. (Photo courtesy of Barney Sterling, Chicago Sports Photographer & Promotions)

"I visited your dad in Good Samaritan Hospital in Phoenix in early March 1971," she said. "That was the only time we met. I can recall nothing about Rube's appearance that gave away how ill he was. It was a shock to learn of his passing a few weeks later, right before the team broke training camp."

Mary didn't have much to offer as far as memories of my dad, but she painted a picture of the Cubs culture. She provided me with context by showing me the Cubs' world my father lived in.

Mary was an oasis. Her voice nurtured me. She searched through her Cubs memorabilia and found some pictures of my dad.

We began a regular correspondence. Among the Cubs and Chicago talk, we would slip in things about ourselves. I confided in her that while my journey to find my dad was for the most part successful, I was struggling in my personal life. She listened.

I couldn't sleep. I had some deep sadness masquerading as anger that was threatening to blast me right out of the trusting metaphorical current. I continued to manage my household, job and kids, but I didn't know how to handle the emotions that were surfacing. I would lay in bed at night once my day was done and yearn.

Dear Yearning,
You drift in and out of me.
I feel you in that soft space between my heart and stomach.
A quiet arrival announced by a wish.
I wish I could bury my head in his chest and smell him.
Hear him say, "you did good" even though I didn't.
You spin me up in fantasy,
You leave me hungry
Because of you I have fed myself with foolish unsatisfying
confectionery

Thirst and lust give way to dehydration and shame.
No more of you. I'm done.
LA

I took a self-imposed sabbatical from the search for my father and started going to yoga and acupuncture in an attempt to exorcise these demons. I had brought it all to the surface, there was no turning back. I wanted the anger, sadness and fear out of me immediately. I just felt stuck.

When I took a break from my dad, I started to feel normal again. I thought I had banished the demons, but they had just gone dormant.

One afternoon a few months later I pulled out my baseball notebook.

There was one name that I had not yet called, Phil Regan. Phil was a Cubs' pitcher from 1968 to 1972. I felt compelled to call him that afternoon and left him a message. It was just 15 minutes later when he called me back.

"Hey, Leigh Ann, this is Phil. When I think of your dad the first thing that comes to mind is his sense of humor," he said.

Phil told me a story of the time the team bus was rolling into New York City and as it went through one of those tunnels that delve deep into the city, my dad stood up and told all the rookies, "If you want to blend in, don't smile. The minute you smile they know you aren't from around here."

He was trying to lighten the mood, especially with the younger guys. They were usually nervous. My dad wanted to remind them they were playing a game for a living. They should have fun doing it.

I enjoyed talking to Phil. He is still involved in baseball with the Mets organization. Phil recommended I call Fred Claire, who had been involved with the Los Angeles Dodgers for decades and was the team general manager from 1987 to 1998. I called Fred.

Fred did not remember my father, but he explained to me that baseball during this time was much like a fraternity. It was smaller and the players had greater access to each other.

He encouraged me to not limit myself to contacting only Cubs players, explaining that any player in the National League at that time could have met and known my dad. It was great advice. Fred also encouraged me to document my journey for a book. Writing a book had not occurred to me. Who would be interested in this?

Fred Claire, Phil Regan and Mary Deese were insistent that I contact former Cubs' traveling secretary, Blake Cullen, who told me my favorite story about my dad.

"Your dad went out of his way to make life easy for the new people," Blake said.

As traveling secretary for the Cubs, Blake had to lug briefcases, stat books, and a portable electric typewriter to all the away games. It was more than one man could humanly carry.

Blake had just been hired by the Cubs and was trying to execute his new job to perfection. With both hands full, he walked to the airport gate to check in the team. My dad came up behind him and without saying a word, took the typewriter.

Now this was the 1960's and a typewriter was about the size of a microwave oven. My dad took it from Blake and carried it to the overhead compartment above Blake's seat on the plane. When they arrived at the hotel, my dad, with typewriter in hand, asked, "What room are you in?" He carried the typewriter to Blake's hotel room door.

From then on at every away game, my dad would send a bat boy to the stands in the 8th inning to fetch Blake's typewriter and bring it to him in the dugout. My dad would then carry the bulky thing back to the hotel for Blake and bring it back again the next day.

Blake told me, "That's just the kind of guy your dad was."

Then he said it again.

"He went out of his way to make life easy for the new guys."

My dad was a selfless guy who observed a need and helped. He didn't require accolades or acknowledgment. He just did what needed to be done because it was the right thing to do. It was kindness for the sake of kindness. It was just more evidence that my dad was a good man.

I certainly didn't blame him for getting sick but I started to see a pattern in my thinking. I would find out something about my dad, it would make me happy, then angry, then sad. I cycled through those emotions with every piece of information I found. It was the way I processed it after all these years. I only recognized the pattern because I was writing it down.

I visited the typewriter story over and over in my mind. I visualized it. Then I cycled through my emotional process. If he did that for a stranger, imagine what he would have done for me.

It always seemed to go the same way. Initially after talking to someone who knew my father, I was content. It was reaffirmed time and time again that my father was a good person. I felt compelled to share the story I had just learned with someone, but within hours I would go quiet. The content and warmth would turn into a clenched jaw. I wouldn't speak the story. A few days later I felt physically ill, exhausted. When I think of the story it sickens me.

That was pretty much the pattern I went through with each piece of information I got.

I just happened to be sitting alone in a quiet house when former Cubs outfielder Jim Hickman returned my call. His slow Tennessee drawl and gentle cadence pierced straight through to my heart. It was a voice similar to my father's.

"Leigh Ann, this is Jim Hickman. Your dad was one of the nicest people I ever met," he said. "All the players loved him."

Jim continued, "He kept everyone laughing."

"Did he ever argue with anyone or not get along with someone?" I asked.

"Goodness, no. I can't imagine anyone not liking him," Jim replied.

I decided to probe a little deeper.

"So, Jim, how did you feel about Leo (Durocher)?" I asked.

"I loved Leo," he said. "He was good to me even after I left baseball and went back to farming. He kept in touch with me. Leo liked your dad, too."

"I've heard that. What did he do to win Leo over?"

"Rube was a hard worker," Jim said. "Everything he did was pure class."

I was getting the hang of asking questions and Jim was easy to talk to. His southern accent just slayed me. I kept him on the phone for at least 45 minutes. He told me about his grandchildren, his iPad he couldn't "get to work" and, of course, we talked about the Cubs.

Jim Hickman died a year later on June 25, 2016. His nickname was "Gentleman Jim." I cherish the conversation I had with him and can still remember the sound of his voice.

Later, I found a newspaper article from years earlier in which Hickman credited my dad with helping him with his swing which improved his hitting.

One of the most unexpected connections I made was with Greg Carlton, the Cubs' batboy while my dad was coach. Greg was unpacking boxes from a recent move and came across a picture of my dad. He did a Google search on "Verlon Walker" and found my blog. He wrote this to me:

"I was a bat boy off and on for eight years for the Cubs. Starting a couple of games in 1964 to full uniform in 1966-1973. Your dad was always my favorite coach. When I would arrive at the field I would always get dressed and run out and shag balls for your dad as he hit balls during infield practice. He would always greet me with, "Here comes my fishing buddy." He once asked me what I used to catch fish with. I told him "worms." I think he got a good laugh out of that. Your dad had a normal voice, not too high pitched yet clear and strong. He was always outgoing and friendly. During his last year with the Cubs as he was dying I remember the food caterers delivering split pea soup in an Igloo aluminum container to the clubhouse with Styrofoam cups to eat out of. I thought, "How cheap." But your dad approached the soup and said out loud, "I love that split pea soup, boy it's good." I don't believe he was being sarcastic, I believe he was happy to be still alive and grateful for anything that before he might not have been so happy with. I have some old films of the Cub's and even a photo of me and your dad as I shagged balls for him in Busch Stadium that I will try to include. But don't worry, your dad's voice was just great. I was 11 when my grandfather died and barely remember his voice, but my mother bought me a tape recorder and years ago I found a tape that he had made telling me about a hunting trip. I actually don't know where that tape is now but can remember his Ozark Mountain accent, slow and methodical. Still imprinted on my mind."

I sat in the parking lot of the grocery store reading his email. My dad interacting with a kid. I was frozen. I couldn't go in the store. I couldn't leave the parking lot. I just sat there with the bat boy and cycled through my feelings. I had to talk to this guy.

Greg began by telling me that Yosh Kawano, the Cubs' clubhouse manager had hired Greg during spring training. I have a photo of myself as a baby sitting on Yosh's lap. I had tracked him down, too, and mailed him a letter with a copy of the picture, but had not heard from him.

One of the first things Yosh had told Greg: Never tell anyone anything that goes on in this clubhouse. Never. Ever.

"What happens in the clubhouse stays in the clubhouse," I said joking.

"Absolutely," said Greg. "I have some great stories that will never be told."

"I have no doubt. Do you have any about my dad?" I inquired.

"The summer before your dad passed, (pitcher) Joe (Decker) was pulled off the mound during a game by Durocher," Greg said. "Leo continued to read him the riot act all the way to the dugout. As we sat in the clubhouse after the game only one person went over to talk and comfort Joe, who had his head buried in his hands – your dad."

"Did he console him?" I interrupted.

"Your dad talked to Joe out loud so everyone could hear, patting him on the back trying to calm his distress. Your dad would have treated you the same way. That's who he was and who he would have continued to be had he lived."

Greg paused, waiting for me to say something, but I couldn't.

"Your dad would be very proud of you," he said simply.

Those words felt so good. Would he be proud though? I was uncertain. I think he would be proud of my determination and seeking, but my life had been plagued with missteps.

I could use some fatherly wisdom right about now.

That relaxed floating in the current feeling I spoke of earlier was gone. The dormant demons were back. I was having trouble eating, I hadn't slept through the night in months. I missed appointments. I made mistakes at work. I was disconnecting from people and quite frankly I wanted to go back to being numb. I had pulled all this grief right up to the surface and I was afraid it was going to destroy me.

"You can be confident that your father was a whole man, kind yet strong, Greg continued. "He was very special to me and to others. I could not say that of the other coaches as I viewed him from a child's perspective. I remember your dad being there one year and I came back the next and he was gone. I knew what had happened but asked Yosh anyway. And he just shook his head and said it was sad."

A 12-year-old observes behavior and situations unclouded by ego and insecurities. The batboy was invisible to some, an errand boy to others, but to my dad he was a wide-eyed kid who loved baseball. I got to see my dad through his eyes, crystal clear and simple. It had never even occurred to me to track down the batboy associated with the Cubs. I think this connection was divinely inspired.

The last person I talked to was Billy Williams, the Cubs' iconic outfielder and Hall of Famer who played 16 seasons in Chicago. He was named an All-Star six times, hit 392 home runs, but never once reached the postseason with the Cubs.

"Hey, Leigh Ann, this is Billy Williams returning your call," he said.

Thank you so much. I was just wondering if you remember my dad, Verlon Walker?

"Everybody called him Rube. I remember him well. He was mild mannered. All the players respected him. When he spoke, we listened," he said. "He didn't rant and rave and he was funny. He had a great sense of humor."

I had gotten used to hearing how funny and kind he was. Billy was just reinforcing what others had already said. I never got tired of hearing it. I felt like while they talked about him, they held him in their mind as I listened and visualized what they told me. It was about as alive as I could make him.

Then Billy told me about visiting my dad at the hospital in Arizona during spring training. He remembers walking over to my dad, lying in the hospital bed. My dad reached out for Billy's hand and squeezed it tight.

"He died about a month later," Billy said. "It was sad."

All these years later Billy remembered the hand squeeze.

Billy asked about my mom. His wife and my mom knew each other. He was happy to know she was well.

It was yet more affirmation that my dad had left an impact on the people around him. Whether it was a teenage batboy, a new team statistician, a journeyman player or a Hall of Fame player, they remembered him and that made me smile. His legacy was his wit and kindness.

I saved all the newspaper clippings I could find about my dad. They were all special in their own way because each added another layer, another dab of color to the picture that made up Verlon Walker.

One particular newspaper clipping has stood out for me. It was written April 4, 1971, by Rick Talley, a columnist for the old *Chicago Today* which would later be absorbed into the *Chicago Tribune* where Talley would become sports editor.

Talley was writing from the Cubs' spring training headquarters in Scottsdale, Arizona. In early April, the optimism was flowing. After all that's what spring training for every team was about. Every team had the same record, the same expectations, the same dreams. Eventually reality would hit, but in the spring, all was right with the world.

In this particular column, Talley was predicting that the Cubs would win the pennant that season because they had everything a championship needed; hitting, pitching, defense and the highest payroll in the National League.

One thing they no longer had was Verlon Walker.

Let him tell the story:

Last September, when the Cubs were blowing it again in Philadelphia, those near the team found different ways to endure the experience.

Two of my friends, baseball writer George Langford and the late Verlon (Rube) Walker, threw a private party. Just the two of them...Langford, one of those good old boys from Tennessee, and Walker, the pride of Lenoir, N.C., coach for the Cubs.

And some sour mash whiskey.

"It was a good party," recalled Walker later. "I wish you could have been there. I can't remember all the details. But I do know I had this depth-finder for fishing, and I remember George filling up the hotel room bathtub so we could test it."

Walker, as most of you know, died 10 days ago from leukemia at age 42. He was one of the warmest human beings I have ever known.

He was the wit of the Cubs and often the heart. He was the man who always said the right thing at the tense moment...the man who dashed into a free-for-all at Wrigley Field last summer for one reason: to shield rival (Pittsburgh Pirates) Manager Danny Murtaugh, who recently has suffered a heart attack.

As a player, Rube was average. Probably less than average as a pro. He never made it to the major leagues...but he could tell you how he beat out the late heavyweight champion Rocky Marciano when they were youngsters in the low minors. Rube always claimed that when Marciano realized he was a worse catcher than him, it made Rocky so furious he went out and started beating up on everybody.

It was in spring training, five years ago, that Walker first learned he had leukemia. For the last several years all of the players and writers with the Cubs had also known.

But thru it all, Rube remained the same. Always talking about the champion hog-caller from Lenoir ("He could call the bacon out of a bacon-lettuce-and-tomato sandwich at 100 yards"), or about his 19-foot fiberglass boat, or about his new home on the lake in the Carolina hills.

"Come on down next winter, and let's go fishing," he'd say every year...but I didn't make it to Lenoir, and for that, I'm sorry, too.

The 1971 Cubs did not win the pennant. They ended up tied for the third place with the New York Mets in the National League East, 14 games behind the eventual World Series champion Pittsburgh Pirates.

I don't know what impact my dad could have had on that with his home-spun stories of Lenoir, his easy nature, his calm demeanor, his ability to find the good in everything. It could have been enough to make up those 14 games and bring the Cubs a title. His significance was not measured in trophies.

His death evoked such an outpouring of compassion, as if all that he had given them was being recycled into the world. These stories about Dad were little healing time capsules held in waiting, left here by my dad finding their way to me when I was ready for them.

A baseball collector, Kevin LeFevers, who lives in my hometown of Lenoir, came to my mom's house one day with an 8 x10 color photograph of my dad. In this image, I could clearly see his ice blue eyes. I stared at them. I had always been jealous of my cousins who would talk about my father's beautiful eyes because they had seen them in person.

When I looked at the picture, I imagined him saying something funny, bragging about his hometown, giving baseball advice, taking care of a situation, consoling someone, looking at me. I began to pull him off the photo paper and into my heart.

That's when he came to me in a dream.

We were sitting in a blue pickup truck drinking coffee. He was wearing a light brown hunting jacket with a dark brown corduroy collar. One hand on the wheel the other holding a Styrofoam cup. Steam rising. He was laughing. It felt real. It was warm like flesh and breath.

I thought about him all the time. I created him, now I missed him. I was not prepared for that.

I began to unravel.

> Dear Dad,
> I miss you. I know I've said all my life that I don't, but
>   now I do.
> I have finally seen your blue eyes, I've heard your voice,
>   I've read your love letters and I dreamed of you.
> The dream felt so real.
> Can you see what it's doing to me?

I feel lost. Crazy. Out of control

I've been really mad at God. Really mad. Can you help
*   with that?*

Come back and visit me in my dreams

LA

PS. I know you sent that bat boy

CHAPTER 6
An End, and a Beginning

The only man I have ever needed left while I still needed him. Verlon Walker was promoted to pitching coach of the Chicago Cubs for the 1971 season. It had been his dream job and after years of wandering through the minor leagues as a coach and player and helping other kids reach their dream, his time had finally come.

He reported to spring training in early February but was hospitalized soon after arriving. In early March, he flew back to Wesley Memorial Hospital in Chicago where he would die later that month. He never got to be pitching coach or be my dad.

Without my father, I had no ground, no gravity. I floated through life without that invisible force holding my feet to the earth. Cascading softly through the stratosphere, twisting gracefully, somersaulting with wispy glittering elegance like a star. Ethereal. A little lost star.

I was all sparkly on the outside but my insides were dark. I've always had the astonishing ability to go numb when needed. It was my survival mechanism. Now, my insides were a mess and I was feeling everything.

The protection I had counted on for so many years was

gone and now I was facing the pain all by myself. Why had I done this? I should have just left well enough alone like my grandmother had suggested many years before.

It was like opening Pandora's Box. Once the box was opened, all that swirled around me was pain, anger, confusion, neediness, fear, sickness, shame, exhaustion. I had unleashed it all.

Nothing was the same. In the myth of Pandora's Box, Pandora slams the box shut before one small, timid spirit could escape – hope.

I felt just like that, all the ills and no hope. It was dark. I was embarrassed. That which I had sought had sickened me. Nobody was going to believe or understand this. I needed to either figure out how not to feel again or navigate a path to survival. I was going to have to give myself ground.

As a child, I developed emotional anesthesia and dosed myself as needed. At my sixth birthday party, a kind woman with frosted pink lipstick leaned in close and told me my father was needed in heaven and that's why God took him.

"Impossible," I thought. "There is no way God needs him more than I do."

There was really no good explanation, but I think it made her feel better to say it, so I smiled. That was the inception of a people-pleasing sickness that would eat away at me for decades.

My mom and I attended a support group after my father died called "Parents Without Partners." It's a nonprofit organization committed to supporting single parents. It was mostly grief therapy camouflaged as a social event held in a church basement. At least that's what I remember. I also remember that the kids and grown-ups were separated into different rooms.

We were a rag-tag bunch bound by our grief and not much else. I managed to connect with one girl. She was outgoing and I was terribly shy. We didn't discuss how our fathers died. I've always found that people who have experienced the death of a parent aren't particularly interested in how the parent died. We don't ask that question, but it is the first question people who haven't directly dealt with death will ask.

We never talked about the suicides, illnesses or accidents. I wasn't alone in avoiding the feelings. We were all masters at pretending to be fine – the kids and the grown-ups.

Weeks earlier I had gotten in trouble at school because I refused to do my work. When pressed by the teacher to do the math worksheet, I just sat there in my pretty purple velvet dress and pig tails and made a bunch of straight lines in the answer blocks.

At one of the Parents Without Partners' meetings, I told my new friend that story. She laughed out loud at my defiance. It was a knowing laughter and I welcomed her into my heart for it.

Dear Defiance,
You are the passive-aggressive blood relative of anger.
I feel you in my legs as I stand my ground.
Pulling brawn from the balls of my feet through my calves
*   and into my taut thighs.*
You don't settle you move up and down my legs.
A contemptuous bravado flails out behind you like a cape
*   tied with strings of deep red spite.*
Disregard is your sidekick.
You helped me not give a damn and feel falsely strong.
I like you
LA

Watching my other girlfriends interact with their fathers was painful. It brought up a guilt-laden jealousy of which I was ashamed. I preferred the company of my broken friend where there would be no father-daughter situations.

I was also not jealous of father-son relationships. An interesting thing happened in fifth grade. A boy that lived in my neighborhood called me. It was a simple conversation lasting only a few minutes. He asked me to come outside and ride bikes with him. I went. I felt like I had been set free. Conversations were easy with him. He didn't ask me questions about my dad – or anything else for that matter.

Our time together was action packed. We played with dogs, rode bikes, went swimming and hit a tennis ball against my house. It was gloriously easy. When his dad was around, I wasn't jealous of their relationship. I actually cultivated my own relationship with his father. Most importantly, my new friend boy wasn't going to invite me to spend the night.

I didn't like to spend the night away from my mom because I was afraid she would die while I was gone. Those were dramatic thoughts for an adolescent which I kept to myself. I tried a few times to spend the night with my girlfriends. The slumber party is practically a rite of passage for the middle school girl. Inevitably, I would call my mom at midnight saying, "Please come get me. I'm homesick."

In my mind, the worst was possible. If she left or died, I would be alone in the world. Who would take care of me? As a result of my bizarre meshing with my mother, combined with an avoidance of any daddy-daughter situations, I found my friend pool dwindling to boys. There was tranquility in the lack of intimacy.

Then puberty arrived and turned the boys into vultures. What followed, predictably, was a murky jumbled mess of emotions, flirtations, and expectations. I quickly adapted to my new role in boy world.

I found that I rather enjoyed the attention I got. It filled my man-sized abyss with a tingly excitement. My step-father branded me "boy crazy." It pains me to say this, but he was right. I would have a string of relationships, one right after the next. I controlled the ending of each one. The minute I perceived trouble, real or imagined, I ran.

Alcohol would carry me through each relationship transition. Seven years of booze and boys stripped my insides bare. There was no external damage. I was a party girl who managed to graduate college with honors. I had plenty of friends, no DUIs, no arrests, no unpaid bills, but the charade was killing me.

The day I checked out of rehab, I walked into the counselor's office wearing the same dark glasses I wore when I walked in 28 days before. He needed my signature on the discharge papers. I took the pen and made one long straight line, just like on the math worksheet 12 years before.

The counselor said to me, "People as defiant as you don't stay sober."

I smiled, thinking about how my "Parents Without Partners" friend had laughed at my defiance a decade earlier.

I got up and walked out, tears rolling down my cheeks from under those glasses. I was secretly afraid he was right. I knew the defiance was just a veil for anger. It was either going to propel me forward or blow me up.

By some miracle, I stayed sober. I went back to school. I found a job and I got married. In the years to follow I would have two boys, Walker and Christopher. Being a mother came easy to me. I was consistently emotionally available for them in a way I had never been for anyone. They showed me my capacity to love which initiated the quest to get to know my father.

I was not prepared for the whirlwind that followed.

A lifetime of unresolved grief was churning inside me while I pretended to be fine. I concluded that I would go to Chicago for the cliché of closure. Closure being a resolution designed to make me feel better. I was certain a pilgrimage to "The Windy City" would heal me.

I booked a flight for a weekend in August, 2015 before my kids went back to school. I would fly up Friday morning and return Sunday afternoon. The Cubs were playing the Braves that Saturday at Wrigley.

I had three objectives. I wanted to go to Wrigley Field where my dad worked. I wanted to see the Rube Walker Blood Center at Northwestern Memorial Hospital, named for my father after his death, and I wanted to meet some of the people in Chicago who helped me, my team. I had to do it all in 48 hours.

Sue Sarcharski, the archivist at Northwestern Memorial Hospital, came across my blog while researching Ernie Banks for an article she was writing.

This is her email to me:

> Hello Leigh Ann,
>
> I recently came across your website, Baseball Love Story, while preparing a remembrance of Ernie Banks for Northwestern Memorial's digital news site. As I perused your pages with great interest, I took particular note of your story concerning the Verlon "Rube" Walker Blood Center here at Northwestern.
>
> I was happy to see that you had early press releases and articles to illustrate your story, and wondered if you had received a reply to your anonymous request for additional information on the Center.
>
> I thought you'd be interested to know that the NM Archives holds a collection documenting the establishment and early years of the Verlon "Rube" Walker Leukemia Center. Some materials came from the Blood Center's own files, while other items such

as press releases, photographs, brochures and event ephemera originated in Public Relations files. I've scanned a small sampling of items from the collection in the attached PDF so you have a sense of what's here. I hope it brings you smiles instead of tears…especially today. (More on that later).

As you know, the Friends of the Rube Walker Leukemia Center eventually joined with other Cubs and White Sox organizations supporting Northwestern like Cubs Care and the Chicago Cancer Baseball Charities, but it's noteworthy that the Center established in your father's name is still carrying on more than forty years later – a great tribute to your father, mother and their many friends in baseball.

I believe in karma, kismet, the Holy Spirit or whatever forces sometimes brings people together for

Another photo of me at Chicago's Wrigley Field in 2015. It was a chance for me to not only to see the place where Dad coached but to go to the blood center at Northwestern University Hospital that bears his name. The Rube Walker Blood Center was created by the Cubs in 1971 to honor him. Mom and I will forever be grateful. (Photo courtesy of Johnny Burbano Photography)

good. Finding your story online has special significance for me, apart from my professional duties as archivist at NM.

On March 24, 1982, my father died in a car accident on his way home from a business trip to South Bend, Indiana. I had just turned 24, so at least there were memories – visual and aural – to comfort my family and me in our loss. My dad was born and raised on the North Side, so naturally he grew up a Cubs fan. When he moved his family to the Southwest Side to be closer to his job, we learned to endure the grief from our White Sox neighbors while rooting for our beloved Cubs.

I have strong memories of listening to Jack Brickhouse's play by play as background noise in our house. Growing up with the Cubs, the name Verlon "Rube" Walker was familiar to me long before I began my career at Northwestern.

I hope your journey to know more about your father will continue and look forward to reading your postings. When I think of my father today, it won't be of his sudden passing. Instead, I'll remember us grabbing our mitts and playing catch after dinner as the summer sun set; of sitting patiently on a curb at the end of the block waiting for his car to come into view so he could give me a "ride home" from work; of his beautiful singing voice and guitar playing; and of cuddling in the well of his legs as he sat crossed-legged in front of the television watching the '69 Cubs together.

Please feel free to contact me if you'd like more information on the collection – I have duplicates of a number of photos and other items that I'd be happy to share with you. So glad to have connected.

I contacted Sue after receiving her email. We began a regular correspondence. She was the first person I called when I was planning the trip to Chicago. I wanted her to go to the Cubs game with me.

I booked a hotel in walking distance of Northwestern with a view of Lake Michigan. I began reaching out to the people who helped me on my journey to set up meetings.

I hired a professional photographer, Johnny Burbano, to take some images of me with my new friends. I confided in Johnny that I wanted a unique portrait of myself at Wrigley. Something unexpected; something I could show my kids. He said he would figure it out. With that, I left the details to him.

In the meantime, I had been contacted by Doug Smith, a writer for MLB.com, who was interested in doing a short video about my story.

When I told him I was planning a trip to Wrigley and The Rube Walker Blood Center, he decided to send a film crew to meet me there. I let MLB and Northwestern work out the particulars. I was sure there would be some sort of HIPAA compliance that would stop the process. Much to my surprise, everything worked out and cameras were allowed in the hospital.

Sue picked me up at the airport Friday morning. We were on our way to a center named for my father, to meet a film crew sent by major league baseball. It seemed impossible. I loved having Sue with me. Besides being a terrific tour guide, she calmed me.

When we arrived at the Rube Walker Blood Center, I touched the metal sign, running my fingers over the top of each letter. It did exist. It was real.

A picture of my dad in the waiting area in his Cubs uniform was the first thing I saw when I opened the door. My dad would be so honored. People come here to get better in the place named after him.

Just like that, Pandora lifted the lid and let hope out of the box. Hope is right here on the eleventh floor of Northwestern Memorial Hospital at the Rube Walker Blood Center.

Standing at the back of the center, I took it all in. Blue curtains hung on tracks to partition off a treatment area. There was a hallway full of doors to private treatment rooms that are filled with expensive equipment. There's a nurses' station in the middle.

My film crew was waiting. The staff welcomed me. Sue refused to be on camera, so there I stood alone with nothing to say. I had prepared nothing. Shocking, I know.

One of the nurses suggested that I talk with a patient. I considered it a privilege to be invited into someone's therapeutic journey.

When leukemia patients come to the center, they sit for hours hooked up to a machine called a centrifuge. The machine cycles out leukemia cells and replaces them with healthy cells. This type of treatment was in its early stages when my father was diagnosed. Today, it saves many lives.

"I feel lucky," the patient said to me. She was a petite woman with no hair and big round eyes. "This place is saving my life," she continued. Her husband sat next to her smiling.

They were both bravely enduring the treatment – just like my parents had done 40 years before. But now technology was on their side.

As I was leaving, the receptionist said, "I want you to know that many of our patients remember your dad as a coach. They mention it when they check in."

This was my dad's legacy. As important as baseball had been in his life, as much time, effort, sweat and toil he had put into that game, it no longer defined him – at least not in my mind. A solution to the disease he had quietly suffered with was his legacy.

Sue dropped me off at The Billy Goat Tavern located in the underbelly of Michigan Avenue. I was meeting my mentor and favorite baseball historian George Castle for lunch.

The restaurant was made famous when the owner, William Sianis, tried to take his pet goat to Game 4 of the 1945 World Series between the Cubs and Detroit Tigers at Wrigley Field. Phillip K. Wrigley, the owner of the Cubs, made Sianis and his pet goat leave the stadium.

As he left, Sianis placed a curse on the Cubs, The Curse of the Billy Goat, which is why they had not won a World Series in 108 years. If you believe in that kind of stuff.

George was quite sure my dad would have eaten at this tavern and suggested we meet there. When the present-day owner found out I was the daughter of a former Cubs coach he wouldn't allow me to pay. I am a coach's daughter, I thought to myself.

While I was checking into my hotel, Johnny, the photographer I hired, called to tell me he had gotten passes to get on the field before the game the following day. His portrait idea was for me to pose sitting in the Cubs dugout.

I was speechless.

That night I walked to Mary Deese's apartment, which was coincidentally six blocks from my hotel. She cooked dinner for me. I slipped my shoes off and put my feet up on her sofa, laying back as if I was visiting an old friend. We talked and laughed for hours.

As I was walked back to my hotel that evening along Lakeshore Drive, a firework show began from The Navy Pier. It was the perfectly timed punctuation to the end of that day. As I strolled alongside the fireworks' reflection in the water, I felt happy and genuinely excited for tomorrow. I was going to Wrigley Field.

The next morning, I met Johnny at the bronze statue of Ernie Banks outside of "The Friendly Confines." I looked up at Ernie in his batting stance. That guy babysat me. Mr. Cub tried to console me when my mom visited my dad in the hospital. Now, I'm staring up at him in bronzed glory.

Being at Wrigley seemed unreal yet perfect at the same time. It had been 35 years since my last visit. Wrigley Field felt smaller than I remember as a 12 year old. Small like when you return to your elementary school and the cavernous hallways have shrunk.

I stared at the iconic scoreboard, touched the ivy, and stood on the third base line. My dad was third base coach for a few years. He would have stood right there. That was his vantage point. Mom would meet him at the bullpen wall near third base and pass me into his arms. He would proudly walk me all around the field. I had been right here with him.

Very few people were at the ballpark. It was quiet. The grounds crew, a few media people, ushers, hot dog vendors were in preparation mode.

Stepping into the dugout, I looked back at Johnny. He said, "Your dad is with you today. I can feel it."

I sat down on the green vinyl cushioned bench. My eyes started to burn with tears.

"Don't!" I said, out loud, as if I could command the tears back down into the ducts. I was not going to cry my eyelashes off in the dugout of Wrigley Field with a photographer's lens in my face. I had not come this far to collapse now.

Yet the little girl in me wanted to lay down on the green vinyl cushioned dugout bench, eye level with the third base line and cry. Let my giant tears hit the cement floor mixing with the spit and dirt of ages. My swollen snotty face pressed against the seat as I heaved my breath in and out. But as a Southern girl, I did my best to hide my tears.

I sat quietly on that green vinyl cushioned bench and smiled for the camera. Pretty much the story of my life.

I used my media pass to visit Pat Hughes in the radio booth. All this started because he was kind enough to throw his support my way. I wanted to hug him, look him in the eyes and thank him. Johnny went with me to capture our first in-person meeting. I stepped into Pat's domain, overlooking the field, and hugged him tightly.

I also met Al Yellon, managing editor of *Bleed Cubbie Blue* and self-confessed bleacher bum. He wrote about me in the popular Cubs blog. He was motivated to do so because of his love for the Cubs. He told me next time I come to Wrigley I have to experience a game in the bleachers. I don't know about that, seems pretty crazy out there.

The Cubs won that day and so did I. My pilgrimage had come together perfectly as if a divine messenger was choreographing the entire thing.

When I returned home from Chicago, I dreamed of Dad again.

I was standing outside Wrigley Field under the famous marquee. It was night. Facing the entrance, I felt the lights from the marquee flashing and blinking above me. My dad appeared in front of the dark opening wearing his uniform minus the hat, smiling.

"I knew if I came here you would, too," I said in my dream.

He walked toward me in a slow easy, motion. Shoulders a bit rounded forward. He was holding something in his left hand. Maybe it was his hat.

I reached out for him thinking, "Finally."

I woke up.

Dear Dad,
*   I started crying when I woke from that dream and I*
*   didn't stop for six months. I didn't cry continuously, of*

course, but I cried every day.
The tears were for you mostly. All the ones I had held in.
There was other sadness too. Sadness I had created.
Why won't you talk to me in the dreams. I want to hear
*   your voice.*
I want to hear it because it would comfort me. I feel
*   terribly uncomfortable and afraid.*
I've never needed you more than I do right now.
Come all the way to me, please.
LA

CHAPTER 7
A Chance to Help Others

The cause of death listed on my father's certificate: Chronic Granulocytic Leukemia known now by the name Chronic Myeloid Leukemia (CML).

CML is a cancer of the bone marrow and blood. A genetic change occurs in the myeloid cell which forms an abnormal gene that turns the cell into a leukemia cell. These sick cells build up in the bone marrow spreading into the blood and sometimes the organs like the spleen. It is a slow growing cancer. Most people can live many years with CML. However, it can become a fast-growing acute leukemia that is hard to treat.

There aren't any known causes except exposure to radiation. As far as I know my father had no exposure to radiation. It is a rare, bizarre disease with symptoms that resemble the flu.

> *Dear CML*
> *Because of you, I hate Father's Day.*
> *You are a complicated, elusive villain*
> *Rare and for the most part slow-growing*
> *You attacked NBA legend, Kareem Abdul-Jabbar, in*
>   *2009. He survived*

*All this time, I've been trying to figure out who to be mad
    at, I think it's you.*
*But that's so unsatisfying. I can't do the normal things
    one does when angry when my opponent is a disease.*
*I can't have a face to face, come to Jesus, tete-a-tete where
    I say a bunch of ugly things that I have to apologize
    for later.*
*I've never been good at that anyway. I'm too afraid of
    confrontation.*
*I can't throw that gift you gave me in the dumpster, then
    tell you via text "I threw the gift you gave me in the
    dumpster." So childish.*
*For now, I will wish for your complete eradication. Rates
    of diagnosis have significantly decreased and survival
    rates have increased.*
That's promising and
*In the middle of the leukemia fight is the Rube Walker
    Blood Center.*
LA

A routine team physical is how my dad learned he had leukemia. He hadn't felt well and just attributed it to exhaustion. The team doctor ran some blood tests and referred him to Dr. Wilson Hartz, a local hematologist, who diagnosed him with leukemia.

My dad shared his diagnosed with Cubs owner P.K. Wrigley, but kept it from most of the players. Not wanting the focus to be on his illness, he continued to coach and show up in a positive way. Many players I spoke with mentioned that they weren't even aware he was sick until he was hospitalized.

After his death the Chicago Cubs made a donation on October 20, 1971, of $35,000 to Wesley Memorial Hospital, now Northwestern Memorial Hospital. My mother and Ernie Banks presented the check to Dr. Hartz, who would be the center's director. This donation established The Verlon "Rube" Walker Leukemia Center. Today it is called The Rube Walker Blood Center or RWBC for short.

The proceeds of an interleague game played on June 24, 1971, at Wrigley Field between the White Sox and the Cubs were donated to the center as well.

The blood center initially consisted of a patient area with two isolation rooms equipped for intensive care, a research lab, and a donor room that housed a centrifuge machine. A centrifuge harvests white blood cells from donors then circulates the red blood cells back to the donor, separating only what the leukemia patient needs. A basic blood transfusion doesn't give a leukemia patient enough white blood cells, but the centrifuge machine could.

White blood cells help the body fight infection and in most blood cancers there are either not enough white cells or too many sick white cells. My father actually died from pneumonia

Some of my favorite people in the world from the Rube Walker Blood Center at Northwestern Hospital that bears my dad's name. They are, from left, Michelle Trudel; myself; Jeanne Martinez, RN; archivist and my favorite Cubs' fan Sue Sacharski; and Megan McCann from the media relations department. It is a place that, quite simply, saves lives every day and I am honored to have my dad's name associated with it.

Finding My Father's Voice

which his compromised immune system could not fight.

The centrifuge was new technology in the 1970s and very few of those machines were available. At the later stages of my dad's illness, he was able to avail himself of a centrifuge at Bethesda Naval Hospital outside Washington, D.C. – the same hospital that was the official health facility for the president of the United States. Unfortunately, by the time he got to use it, his illness was too far along to do much good. Still, it showed doctors in Chicago how effective the technology was and, perhaps more to the point, how much better it would be as time went on.

Due to the Cubs generosity and my father's insistence prior to his death, Chicago residents were able to receive treatment using the centrifuge at the Rube Walker Blood Center. It has made a miraculous difference for thousands of patients over the years. The first year the center performed 150 processes. Today, they average 4,000.

These machines aren't cheap, nor was the care for patients with blood diseases. So, for years the hospital would have a fundraising event for the center which they called "Turnabouts." Chicago Cubs players and coaches made sure they were part of it.

At Turnabouts, players, coaches and staff would be waiters, bartenders and entertainers and serve the attending guests. Typical roles were "turned about." The public could purchase tickets with all proceeds going to the center. There would also be auctions and raffles of baseball memorabilia. Essentially, if you bought a ticket you could have Billy Williams as your bartender and Ernie Banks might perform a song. The events were successful in raising money for the RWBC. Mom and I attended the first few events.

At the last fundraiser Mom and I attended together, I must have been six or seven years old. Mom decided to take a tour of the blood center the day before. We showed up at the hospital and a nice woman took us through going into great detail about the care and treatments. At the end, she turned to my mom and said, "Rube Walker was a coach for the Cubs."

"Yes, I know. He was my husband. This is his daughter," Mom replied.

"I wish you would have told me! I could have introduced you to everyone," the woman exclaimed.

"I just wanted to see the progress. I didn't want it to be about us," Mom explained.

That evening we attended the Turnabout, flying home the next morning.

Sue Sacharski, the hospital's archivist since 1980, has kept all the details of the Turnabouts and recalls only too well how much fun, and how important, they were.

As you can see from my swollen eyes, this had been a long, emotional day for me as I visited the Rube Walker Blood Center at Northwestern University Hospital in 2015. I had heard about this place and I knew what good work they were doing there. I'm standing in front of his photograph that hangs at RWBC. It was overwhelming to finally see it in person and to talk with the people it was helping and to the people who were doing such great work. I know my father's spirit wanders those halls every day. (Photo courtesy of Sue Sacharski)

"These were kind of a big deal locally," Sue said. "The first few years it was a blast."

The Cubs took part for one simple reason: to honor my father.

"Everybody loved Rube," Sue said. "That's what these Turnabout events showed me. These are players and coaches with big egos, but they did skits and talked about Rube. It was a real show of love for the guy. He was never in the forefront with the Cubs, but the Cubs loved him."

When I was 12 years old, I flew to Chicago alone to attend the fundraiser for the Rube Walker Blood Center. I stayed with Dr. Hartz and his wife, Anahise. They had two daughters, Dionne and Melinda, who were close to my age.

I wore a long, cream-colored dress with a lacy shawl. I pulled my hair up to show off some sparkly earrings. Feeling very grown up, I walked into the beautiful ball room. A woman came right over to me and said, "You are Verlon Walker's daughter, aren't you? I brought you something."

She reached in her clutch purse and pulled out a keychain wrapped in soft cloth. Pressing it into my hand she said, "Your dad was a good man. I'm sorry you didn't know him." It was a keychain from the previous year's event. It had my dad's face on one side and words on the other. I didn't read the words right then.

Later I pulled the keychain out of the pocket of my dress and read it. It said, "Think of me now and again, as I was in life at some moment which is pleasant to remember."

My throat felt tight. I kept swallowing and breathing until it didn't feel tight anymore. It wasn't the key chain or the sentiment, or the nice woman that upset me. I was upset because I had no moment "which is pleasant to remember." I could pull nothing up in my mind. Nothing. I was standing in a ballroom full of people who knew him. I didn't know him. I had not one memory of my own. I never went back to the fundraisers.

I am proud to report that the Rube Walker Blood Center thrives.

When I started my quest, I did a Google search to see if the center still existed. I wanted to talk to someone there but wasn't sure what to say. Coincidently, a few months later, Sue Sacharski, the archivist, reached out to me. She opened up a channel of communication with the RWBC. The following information came from staff members at the center. What began as a leukemia center has changed to a blood center that treats many types of blood related illnesses. I asked a staff member to provide me with information regarding the treatments available at the RWBC.

She explained that the RWBC's current procedures include stem cell harvest for treatment of lymphomas, leukemia, multiple myeloma, MS, and other autoimmune disorders as well as transfusions of red blood cells or platelets and electrolyte replacement.

"On a typical day, we may see anywhere from 7-10 stem cell harvest patients along with 20 or so patients receiving other treatments. I think the most important thing to know about RWBC, in addition to the therapies we provide, is that our patients really make coming to work a very easy task.

"We admire the patients we care for because of their strength, courage, and kindness even through the fight they are fighting every day. They are amazing people!"

The program coordinator, Michelle Trudel, told me about a few of the patients. This is what she wrote:

> Young patients with sickle cell anemia who are then able to attend college courses.
>
> A young professional advertising agent with immunodeficiency who receives monthly IV medication in the evening to stay healthy.
>
> An elderly patient not eligible for further

chemotherapy receiving blood and platelet support for his leukemia and staying alive to see his grandchild get married.

Healthy sibling-matched donors willing to share their time and energy to donate life-saving stem cells to their sibling.

Neurology patients who are initially not able to walk because of their diseases and then slowly, steadily improve with apheresis procedures that assist their neurological system to repair (CIDP, MG, MS)

A survivor of the Katrina Hurricane in New Orleans, requires blood transfusions every week. He brings his wife who is suffering from dementia. He brings the only picture they were able to save from their home – a picture of him and his "bride" when they were first married.

Dear Dad,
You must have been full of fear the day you found out you were sick.
Mom said that after I was born you took me to Dr. Hartz for blood tests. You wanted to be sure I wasn't sick too. They know now that it isn't genetic.
From what I have learned about you, I think you are way too humble to care that your name is on a hospital building. You might say, "that kinda thing is for high falutin rich folks."
They have fancy letterhead and ballpoint pens with your name on them.
Benefits were held in your memory to raise money.
Your picture is in the waiting room.
I'm sorry you suffered. I think you were incredibly brave.
LA

CHAPTER 8
Finding the Way Back

W hat was the point? No, seriously, what was it?

I was never going to get what I really wanted, which was my dad in the flesh. It was a profound, significant loss that had changed me. It had shaped the way I saw everything.

Victoria Secunda writes in her book *"Women and Their Fathers"*:

> "Losing a father in childhood forever changes the shape of a daughter's identity – how she views the world and herself. Not only is her connection to the first and most important man in her life sharply extinguished, but all her perceptions, all her decisions, all her future relationships are filtered through that early unimaginable loss."

My data gathering phase was done. I might stumble upon more stories, pictures, or video but I had made him as real as he was ever going to be. It was time to make peace with that.

I had started with a naive yearning for my father. My 42-year-old body encased a fractured little girl. Off I went on my road of trials with no real direction and little preparation. I was going to embrace my father and escape my grief. Surrounded by masculine allies, who advanced my journey, I thrived.

I was thrilled with my success. I basked in the attention. I had absorbed his wit, kindness, illness, eye color and voice into me until I dreamed of him. I had been victorious in the initial journey of finding my father. A secondary journey was forming. I was finding myself.

A descent followed.

Having found my treasure and completing what I thought was my heroic journey, I entered a period of personal chaos. My emotions were erratic, my behavior was impulsive, my grief was overwhelming. Nothing felt the same to me. I no longer fit into the life I had created.

I woke up in the night drenched in sweat, shivering. I paced around my house in the dark, waiting for daylight. Thinking today would be the day I would pull it together, snap out of it. I was no longer dreaming of my dad.

Dear Broken Heartedness
I feel you in my upper back behind my heart.
When I breathe, piercing pain radiates down my arms
    and legs into my hands and feet.
A crucifixion
Unbearable
Exhausted but awake with pain
You placed me in martyrdom
Needy
Pathetic
LA

I went to work but got very little done there. I couldn't remember simple things like names, passwords, pin numbers, directions. I drove in circles, passing turn offs, forgetting how to get to places I had driven to many times before.

Days bled together. I couldn't remember if I talked to my mom that morning or two days prior. I signed up to volunteer at Chris' school and never showed up. I forgot appointments. I asked my kids the same questions over and over. Information wouldn't stick in my mind.

I hit the back of a Ford F150 which was parked at a stop light. Nobody was injured, but I continued to drive my Jeep for the next week, even though the hood was bent up and the front was smashed in. When I took it to the dealership, it was deemed "undriveable." I was sleep walking through my days.

I managed to be on time and at the right location for a holiday lunch with some girlfriends. Walking to my car afterward, one friend approached me basically asking what was up with me. She could tell I wasn't myself. At first, I lied saying I was fine but Christmas might kill me. She gave me the "I'm not buying it" look.

I got in the front seat of her car and began talking. She listened. I don't remember anything that was said that day. I only remember the way she made me feel. I was going to be OK, until it was actually OK. She was going to make sure of it. That was a turning point for me.

The next few months are a blur.

I moved out of my home that I shared with my husband for 19 years and into an apartment about two miles away.

Walking away from the life I knew was frightening. I wasn't sure I could survive on my own and I was positive my children would be broken by the new arrangement of splitting time between my new apartment and the house they grew up in. The details of the demise of my marriage are too personal to discuss here but I felt as if I had failed. I went into a self-imposed period of isolation.

This was a dark time.

My new apartment had a walk-in closet. I would take my pillow and duvet into that closet, lay on the floor with the door shut in the dark for days. It was my chrysalis. Surrounded by my clothes and shoes, which is about all I brought with me from my old life. I sifted through feelings suspended in a peculiar place. I molted. It was terribly uncomfortable. I cried. A lot.

Avoiding the grief had distorted my thinking and triggered all my character defects. Character defects is a 12-Step term referring to shortcomings such as: anger, selfishness, impatience, resentment, laziness. I was coming to terms with how the avoidance of my grief driven by fear had harmed me. I was shedding.

I hid my anger behind defiance. I hid lies behind people pleasing. I hid resentment behind sarcasm. I had a repository of self-loathing because of it. I laid in that closet and wept about it. I knew I had to transform for myself and for my children. It was going to take some time.

Walking into the gated courtyard of my new apartment building, I startled a butterfly from its hiding place in a tree. It flew so close to my face, I felt the wind of its wings on my cheek. It playfully danced around my head in long slow circles.

My eyes followed every movement. I turned my body around to watch it float behind me, then beside me, then away from me. Blackish blue wings with orange edges and tiny white dots glided above me making larger circles up and up and up, until it was gone. I stood there, frozen, straining to see it.

"Come back," I whispered.

It didn't come back. I continued to stand there in hope for several minutes, looking up. I looked with anticipation for that butterfly each time I entered the courtyard for weeks after that.

It had graced me with its whimsy for only a brief moment and was gone.

Seeing the unexpected butterfly was like dreaming about my father. Before the journey, I thought making him real would heal my heart infusing me with confidence. That didn't happen. Just like the butterfly, he whooshed over me. I would never really have him. What I learned is this:

The journey is the treasure.

The point had been to seek my dad and by doing that, I broke myself open. All the sickness inside me came gushing out.

At my core, I felt abandoned by every man I had known. A victim, but I had played the role of abandoner as well. It was a sick back and forth love dance that started at age 3.

As a child, I had limited perspective, so my core belief was: people leave and I'm too weak and sensitive to handle it. I better protect my heart. My brain grew around that belief. An abandonment core is fear-based. Fears impede a person's ability to experience intimacy. It creates anxiety, depression, addiction, self-sabotage, and low self-esteem. My quest had triggered my core issue.

Dear Abandonment
You are always with me.
As much a part of me as my O+ blood.
You make up stories. In irrational fear, you scan for
　evidence to support your lies.
You have sabotaged me again and again
You say to me, "Why love someone, when they are just
　going to leave eventually?"
"You don't need anyone. You can't trust anyone. You are
　alone"
You trick me into creating exactly what I fear the most....

Being alone without my needs met.
You have ruled my life through; depression, fear of
emotional intimacy, repressed anger, self-sabotaging
behavior and feeling like everything was my fault.
Getting rid of you seems impossible, like changing the way
I laugh.
You are my built-in response to stimuli.
If I can't abolish you, let me at least learn to ignore you.
LA

The wrecking ball had come through; my armor was cracked. I had a split-second opportunity to see myself and change before the numbness, abandonment and fear rushed to "save" me. I would rebuild myself as I had built my dad, layer by layer, slowly.

I declared 2016 my rebuilding year.

I began with sleep. I had been operating at a deficit. For the first time in many years, I was alone for significant amounts of time. I shared custody with my husband which meant my boys shuffled back and forth every few days. When I had them, I focused on them. When I didn't, I focused on fixing me.

I had a healthy respect for my addiction during this time. It was whispering to me, "Who do you think you are? You aren't going to get any better, don't bother." Addiction morphs until you don't recognize it.

Dear Addiction,
You are a sickness rooted in the mind skewing my
perception
You wait patiently for an opportunity to trick me
You spin me up in delusion
I feel you in my throat and on my tongue
The sensation of a dry mouth muttering "more"

Peddling tranquility
You will only make trouble here
Back up off me...
LA

During my first days alone, I moved from sofa to bed to sofa and back again. I didn't dress, watch TV, answer the phone or listen to music. I sat quietly in a state of shock looking out the window at the clouds.

The frenzied pace of my life, as a mom working part-time, leading up to my archeological dig for grief had left me weary. The emotional stress of separation pushed me to a state of fragility. I collapsed.

Once I felt rested, I ventured out. I went food shopping at a market in my new neighborhood. I walked up and down the aisles looking for my normal items: almond milk, peanut butter, bananas, club soda. It was disorienting. Everything I did felt like I was doing it for the first time. At my regular market, I could run in and out, blindfolded, in five minutes.

I scheduled one positive activity each day forcing myself out into the world. A yoga class followed by meditation on Sunday mornings became a valuable part of my routine as was a gathering of friends for dinner on Friday evenings. Those activities bookended my weekends. On Saturdays, I tried to do very little. My nervous system needed the solitude.

I was a bit on edge everywhere I went. Nothing felt familiar. It took time for me to build a new daily routine. I called my mom just about every morning to hear her voice. She would say, "Leigh, you can do anything you set your mind to. I've seen you." I needed her to believe in my strength until I could feel it for myself.

I launched a year-long crusade to cure my mind, body and soul. This crusade included acupuncture, reiki, therapy, cleansing, detoxing, meditation, and yoga. I had spent three years surgically removing my pain. I figured I needed at least a year to mend.

I was also having trouble with digestion. It was as if I could not digest all the change in my life and that impacted my ability to eat food. I showed up at my acupuncturist office one afternoon shaky and weak. She looked at my tongue and diagnosed me as deficient.

I set up regular appointments with her to reset my system. She positioned the needles in my body as if she could see through my skin. Turning off the lights, she gently touched my arm saying, "Rest. I'm right outside if you need me."

I laid there on the table in the dark, face down trying to shut down my mind. Sometimes I was successful. Other times I felt like I wanted to jump off the table and run to my car. Acupuncture is powerful medicine. Within weeks my appetite came back.

I decided food was medicine. I began juicing regularly, trying to eat mindfully. My body responded to the good food and extended rest. I felt physically stronger. It was suggested to me that I consciously bless everything I put into my body. Before I ate or drank anything, I tried to say to myself something like "this kale-aid will nourish my body." The blessing brought a positive awareness to everything I ate and drank connecting my mind to my body.

Yoga continued to build on my mind/body connection and grounded me in the present moment. The yoga teacher would often prompt the class to set an "intention" at the beginning of class. The idea behind an intention is to practice the characteristic with yourself on your yoga mat then transfer it into your life. My intention was either "presence" or "healing."

Trying something different, I started using the characteristics I had learned about my dad as my intention at yoga: kindness, integrity, wit and optimism. For example, I would practice optimism as I moved through Sun Salutation sequence. I was being grateful for my healthy body that carried me through the day. My dad was optimistic while facing terminal illness. I used him as inspiration, honoring him with an optimistic attitude. I said to myself: I can do this hard, physical work in class to prove I can do the mental work outside of class.

I went to two different yoga studios every chance I got. I became stronger, more flexible and more patient as my practice advanced. My mind wasn't nearly as strong as my body.

I signed up for a yoga workshop which focused on handstands. I felt like I was strong enough to do a handstand, but I was afraid. My mind was working against my body like mental poison. Fear and negative thoughts had plagued my life. It was apparent, if I wanted to get better, I had to address my thoughts. Doing a handstand was merely symbolic.

Guess what? I did a handstand. I'm no superstar, but I faced my fear and went upside down a time or two which did wonders to counteract my inner dialogue which had been saying, "You can't do that. You will look foolish. Don't even try." But I did that handstand.

Many times, I got off track with negative thoughts. I gathered a small team of women around me as insulation from the world. I took my twisted pessimistic thoughts to them. When I felt insecure, confused or sad, they guided me through the landmines of being alone, of craving attention from men, of dealing with the loss of my dad.

I texted them from the closet, saying "I'm in the closet again." My friend Meredith would offer to come over or go somewhere with me. "I don't want to. Just talk to me," would be the gist of my response. She always would. No matter what she had going on. It helped me not feel so alone.

Drake, the musician/rapper, became the man in my life. He released his studio album "Views" in April 2016, singing about the woes in his rather charmed life, and I identified. It was a mix of cool mood and angry words. Meredith would ask, "What did you do this weekend?" I would reply, "Drake and I went to the pool for a few hours. Then we cleaned the apartment and now we are making food."

When Drizzy's tour came through North Carolina in August, I took Walker. I had purchased the tickets in May, thinking to myself, "By August I will be better." I was implementing my new found positive-thought projection. I was much improved by the concert in August.

I joked that Drake and Tammy Bell, my therapist, got me through summer of 2016.

Therapy gave me self-awareness. I was finally able to identify patterns in my behavior that no longer served me. I had learned as a child that telling people how I felt was risky. They might get angry or feel uncomfortable.

I didn't ask for what I needed. I ran from my feelings, which is why I hid under the weeping willow tree, didn't cry at the ballpark, detached from my dad, and drank those stories away. It all began to make sense.

Tammy Bell who is a Licensed Clinical Social Worker with a Masters in Addiction Counseling and a Certified Relapse Prevention Specialist, gave me a "roadmap" to recovery which involved a continuous awareness of my behavior. I had therapy sessions with her twice a month for a year. This is a life-long battle similar to my addiction. I did exactly what she told me to do. No defiance.

Tammy told me; "Don't be afraid of the pain and grief. It's not going to kill you. It might feel like it, but it won't. Commit to feeling whatever comes up... be like Dory from

Finding Nemo. Just keep swimming. You will learn who you really are."

I went swimming at night at the pool for my apartment complex. I had a pool as a little girl at my grandmother's house. Laying back into the water, letting my body sink just below the surface, I stared up at the stars and moon. With my ears under the water, I could hear my own breath and heartbeat magnified. I would breathe, listen and float just like I did as a little girl at my grandmother's pool. It was my own personal baptism. I found the sound of my breath calming. In turn, that ignited an interest in meditation.

Meditation is by far the most significant component of my healing crusade. It taught me to control my thoughts. I began with two minutes in the morning and evening, adding a minute every day until I reached 15 minutes every morning and evening.

I would sit in a cross-legged position, with eyes closed, and count my breath. I'd breathe in to the count of four, then breathe out to the same count. I noticed right away that my mind was unruly and full of nonsense. I was either reliving past events or worrying about the future. Both scenarios took me right out of the present moment. Connecting to my source requires that I be present in the moment which I found rather difficult. My reiki master gave me the mantra; *Shanti Hum* which means "I am peace." The purpose of the mantra was to give my unruly mind something on which to focus. It worked. For the first time in my life I understood what it meant to have peace of mind.

On August 12, 2016, I decided to try 24 hours of silent meditation. Basically, I spent a day meditating for an hour at a time with 30-minute breaks for resting, eating, stretching or walking. I wasn't allowed to read, talk, listen to music, watch TV. No electronics, no noise. It was just me alone with my thoughts.

As I suspected, I started out strong with a peaceful focus. However, within a few hours the meditation position became uncomfortable. My legs were falling asleep and my lower back was aching. I was distracted by my physical pain, which led to a cavalcade of my problems marching through my mind demanding my attention.

Financial Insecurity came trotting by first. Big, ugly, scary monetary bullies screaming, "You can't support yourself."

Regret stomped through proclaiming, "Remember when you did that? You shouldn't have done that."

Then Shame entered, looking beautiful in a fashionably stunning outfit and calmly stated with precise certainty, "You are bad."

I trudged forward reluctantly, adhering to the meditation schedule I had set up. I battled my mind and body for the next few hours. My legs went numb and my mind was whirling darkly.

I felt like a passenger on a broken down crazy train. The harder I tried, the worse I felt. I considered quitting. "You are a quitter. Just quit," Shame whispered. I took a deep breath and flailed my legs straight out of lotus position lying back on the floor. Relief washed over my physical body. I stared trance-like at the ceiling and this thought floated into my mind:

Struggle no more my sweet girl
I got you.
Relax into me and know I am here.

I rested there, euphoric. I don't know if it was my father, my intuition or just my exhausted body speaking to me.

Once I heard it, my mind went dark. I spent the remaining meditation in a state of profound understanding that I was going to be okay. I could take care of myself, I could seek forgiveness,

I was whole and I am not alone. I felt like a butterfly, free and beautiful.

In Elizabeth Kübler-Ross' book, "On Death and Dying," she created a model on how to process grief concluding that we move through five stages. Freud talked about grief being a long private journey describing it as "work."

I found I didn't fit into the Freud or the Kübler-Ross model.

If you are grieving, expect a multitude of emotions. Grief isn't necessarily a steady process. I have found it to be messy. It constricts and loosens. It stops and starts.

You need to go at your own pace. There is no clock or statute of limitations on grief – just like baseball.

Most importantly, ask for help. It is a solitary journey but team players who are helping are required for advancement.

While I was progressing through my metamorphosis out of my closet and back into the world, another restoration was occurring simultaneously in my hometown of Lenoir at Walker Stadium.

In August 1971, five months after my father's death, Davenport Stadium was renamed Walker Stadium in honor of my father and my uncle. It was quite an event. The New York Mets and the Chicago Cubs, the two teams so closely aligned with the two brothers, sent bronze plaques and a brick memorial was built at the entrance to the stadium.

The plan to dedicate the stadium got its start in 1969 after the brothers played each other in the National League series. A handful of Lenoir baseball fans wanted to honor the two Walker brothers for making it to the big leagues and came up with the idea.

The Kiwanis Club of Lenoir organized the campaign. Over the next two years, beautiful letters of tribute were written and sent to Lenoir from Ron Santo, Don Kessinger, Joe Garagiola and Jack Lang, president of the Baseball Writers Association of America.

In his letter Ron Santo wrote, "Verlon's great concern and passion for his fellow man was without equal. His help is not only educational, but inspirational, with his great wit and wisdom."

Don Kessinger wrote "Verlon has contributed to the success of the Cubs in so many ways, not only is he always available to help the ballplayer but he is a constant source of humor. If the rest of the citizens of Lenoir can be judged by Verlon Walker, it must truly be a wonderful place to live."

Don added a P.S. to the bottom of his letter that read, "I would like to ask Verlon to explain to his fellow citizens why on October 1, 1969, a young lady raced out of the stands right past Verlon to kiss third Mets third baseman, Wayne Garrett. And Verlon is always telling us how good looking he is."

Joe Garagiola wrote, "Congratulations to the Kiwanis Club for honoring the Walker brothers. My thanks to both Verlon and Al because in following their baseball advice, they made me what I am today – a bald-headed baseball announcer. The fact that Verlon was a coach for Durocher tells you something about his courage. Congratulations to two great guys!"

The stadium is nestled in a neighborhood with bungalow brick homes, tree-lined streets with sidewalks. The neighborhood is just blocks from the quaint uptown.

After the dedication, the field was used by many youth leagues, specifically the American Legion Post 29 League which enjoyed a pinnacle of popularity in the late 1980s. My high school boyfriend was a star on the Caldwell County Post 29 team which won the state championship in 1986.

Unfortunately, over the years, Walker Stadium had become a sad shadow of what it used to be, something of an ancient relic from a bygone era. The field was no longer the center of attention in Lenoir. The lights were taken down, weeds overtook the stands, grass grew over the pitcher's mound, the dugouts where falling apart.

When visiting Lenoir, I would take my boys there to run around the overgrown field and up and down the concrete bleachers. It was bittersweet. I felt powerless to do anything about it since I no longer lived in Lenoir. I simply accepted the inevitable march of time.

Then a miracle occurred.

One gorgeous Sunday afternoon, with my mom and my boys in the car, I decided to drive past Walker Stadium. I parked the car and walked toward the front gate. I couldn't believe my eyes.

I saw an actual baseball diamond instead of unkempt, unruly grass. The field had been manicured. There was an actual pitcher's mound. The home team dugout was painted and completely redone. A new press box had been built. There was a new scoreboard, a new back stop, and signs advertising local businesses were hanging on the outfield fences.

A group of local people who felt nostalgic about the place had begun their own crusade to save the ballpark. They raised money and volunteered their time to restore the stadium to its former glory. A labor of love. The field was deemed an asset to Lenoir, a piece of positive history. Baseball was being played there again.

A summer wooden bat league team, the Lenoir Oilers, now make Walker Stadium their home. The Oilers are part of the Carolina-Virginia Collegiate League. The players come from college Division I, II and III, as well as the NAIA and junior college.

Clifton Bennett, a local entrepreneur, purchased the team in 2015. He and his close friend, Kevin Bumgarner, developed a plan to bring the Oilers to Lenoir and specifically to Walker Stadium for the 2016 season. Kevin is the father of San Francisco Giants pitcher Madison Bumgarner, and Clifton is a former player in the semi-pro wooden bat league. They both umpired in the region, so baseball is more than just a pleasurable past time.

Clifton wanted to bring a team to the Walker field and asked Kevin to be the general manager. Kevin said, "I actually thought to myself, how hard can that be?"

I spoke with Kevin one afternoon. He had a sense of humor that immediately put me at ease.

"The field looked like Wild Kingdom," he said, referring to the neglect. "There was a lot of work to do."

He and Clifton managed to gather support from local companies and the community. In their first year, the Lenoir Oilers captured the CLCV Championship which is a testament to the dedication of the organization, support of the fans and maybe the sacred ground on which they play.

While I was on the phone with Kevin he asked me to throw out the first pitch at the season's home opener for the Oilers in 2017. I will represent the Walker family. The coach's daughter throws out the first pitch at stadium named after her father and uncle. I've come full circle.

The stadium is also getting lights with money donated to the city for that purpose. Day games are difficult in the summer heat. Baseball is better at night under lights. In an interesting twist, the person contracted to design and install the lights is my high school boyfriend, the one who played baseball.

I think throwing out the first pitch is an honor. I had a nice text conversation with Kevin about this as I obsessed over whether, even though the genes of a baseball player were a part of me, if I could really do the job.

> Kevin: Remember, you are throwing out the first
> pitch of our entire 2017 season, don't bounce it,
> LOL

Me: I need to practice – don't want to embarrass
   myself
Kevin: There's no need to be nervous. Remember,
   everybody there will be in YOUR house
Me: Gosh—I don't see it that way but I appreciate
   the encouragement.
Kevin: It's Walker Stadium, and actually you will
   notice on everything we do and say it's Historic
   Walker Stadium. I decided the change would be
   fitting before we ever played last year. If you say
   out loud, it sure sounds good.

Yes, it surely does – Historic Walker Stadium!

Here I am standing with the people who helped bring Walker Stadium back to life. Kevin Bumgarner, on the far left, is the Lenoir Oilers general manager and Clifton and Cheri Bennett are the team owners. All three got the community involved in donating money to help refurbish a ballpark that had fallen into disrepair and had, in many ways, simply been forgotten. With the stadium renovated, the Lenoir Oilers joined the Carolina-Virginia Collegiate League in 2016 and the old park is now pulsing with new energy. And I can't think of a better tribute to my father. (Photo courtesy of David Laxton)

What I know is that the new team has breathed life into the abandoned field. It is rich with hope and opportunity instead of destitute with neglect. Historic Walker Stadium and I are works in progress surrounded by love.

Dear Dad,
Look at Walker Stadium!
Look at me throwing out the first pitch.
I thought of you the minute I stepped on the mound.
I practiced throwing, but I bounced it anyway
Just more evidence of the lack of you
Mom, Walker and Chris joined me out there so I didn't
    feel alone
I don't dream about you anymore. I feel you in me though.
    I hear your voice in my head sometimes encouraging
    me. Like when Kevin asked if I would throw out the
    first pitch, I immediately thought "I can't do that".
    Then I heard you say "Oh yes you can"
I think your voice has been there all along, I just had to
    get quiet and confident enough to hear it.
LA

CHAPTER 9
A Journey That Never Ends

N inety seconds. That was all I was probably going to hear of my father's voice. What I had really been searching for was his wisdom, his counsel, his love and myself. My quest had brought me all those things.

I had imagined my father's voice many times as a child. I would listen to men speak and wonder if he sounded like that. When I finally heard my father's voice, it wasn't what I expected. I had thought it would be kind of low and gravelly like my uncles' voices, but on the tape, it was higher pitched, soft and sweet.

Baseball was my dad's life. I found him there, not on the tape. I've always been a baseball fan, following the Cubs even through the rocky years. This journey with my team, my pilgrimage to Chicago, and my personal transformation have shown me that baseball is my living connection to my dad. As a coach's daughter, I want to take you on my baseball adventure.

In 2016, I had a love affair with the Chicago Cubs. This was the year the Cubs finally won the World Series after 108-year drought. Like myself, the Cubs had just gone through a metamorphosis and is was time we both enjoyed the fruits of our labor.

The Cubs began a renewal when the Ricketts family, led by Chairman Thomas Ricketts, purchased the team in 2009 from the Tribune Company. No one really thought too much about it since the team had been bought and sold before. Every new owner would peddle the promise of home. They began with a costly renovation and preservation of Wrigley Field.

The players came and went in a blur, as did the managers from Lou Piniella to Mike Quade to Dale Sveum and Rick Renteria. The team wasn't much better during this time.

After the 2011 season, the Cubs hired Theo Epstein as the team's new president. Epstein was the wunderkind who had taken another franchise with decades of frustration to the top. He was the architect of the Boston Red Sox winning two World Series in a three-year span. Ricketts hoped he could work the same magic in Chicago.

In the course of the next three years, Epstein made many deals and supplemented the farm system with an eye toward the future. That included a harsh and unceremonious ousting of Renteria as manager after just one season in 2014 to make room for the "king of cool" Joe Maddon.

Joe Maddon, a clever and eccentric baseball man, was let go by the Tampa Bay Rays. Epstein jumped at the opportunity to hire him. He was the veteran presence in the dugout that these young players needed. In 2015, led by Maddon, the Cubs roared to the National League Championship Series but were swept away by the New York Mets.

Syndicated columnist George F. Will, who has written lyrically about baseball for decades, is a long-time Cubs fans and has famously stated, "Cubs fans are ninety percent scar tissue."

I can relate. Every year fans proclaim, "This is the year!" And every year, the disappointment is palpable. At the start of 2016, there was reason for the hope and enthusiasm. This team really was that good. There was something different about 2016 for me and the Cubs. Our scar tissue was overshadowed by a pure positive desire to succeed.

For my birthday on April 1, a friend gave me my own **W** flag and a Roku, a streaming TV and media player. The **W** flag is a white flag with a big blue "W" that hangs at Wrigley when the Cubs win. I would hang mine on my balcony. From my home in Charlotte, North Carolina, I downloaded MLB.com onto my Roku so I could watch all the Cubs games. The home opener was April 11. I was ready.

In the first week of baseball but before the home opener at Wrigley, Kyle Schwarber, a clutch player from last season, had collided with teammate Dexter Fowler and injured his knee. Schwarber was out for the season. He was one of the vanguards of this young, talented team. In just 69 games in 2015, Schwarber had hit 16 home runs and in the postseason, he hit five more as the Cubs knocked off both the Pirates and the hated Cardinals before losing to the Mets.

A week into the season and a key element was gone. The negative chatter began. The Cubs have been cursed by a billy goat and a black cat. All their bad luck can be traced back to those two animals.

The black cat incident happened in 1969 when my dad was a coach. The Cubs entered September in first place. It seemed they were on their way to ending what, even then, was an ancient streak of futility.

Then on September 9, while playing the Mets at Shea Stadium, a black cat wandered onto the field and walked by the visitors' dugout right past Ron Santo, who was in the batter's box.

When that incident occurred, the Cubs still in command of the division. They held a 17 ½-game lead over the Mets but it all slipped away. The Cubs with third base coach,

Verlon Walker, would lose eight games in a row while the Mets with pitching coach Rube Walker, won 10 in a row.

The black cat caused what is referred to as the *Cubs Collapse*. The Mets went on to win the division and, eventually the World Series, calling themselves the *Miracle Mets*.

There were plenty of legitimate reasons for the Cubs falling apart in 1969, not the least of which they stopped hitting and pitching. Much of the blame also fell on manager, Leo Durocher, who refused to give key players a break during the stretch run. Several players, exhausted from a long season, simply wore out as did the pitching staff.

I would love to know what my dad thought of that season as he watched it slowly crumble. I imagine he used his sense of humor to tell the players to calm down, do what you do best, don't worry about all the outside stuff and just play the game.

I refused to buy into the negative conversations about Schwarber as I settled in to watch the Cubs' home opener of the 2016 season. With 40,882 fans in attendance and WGN reporting the highest TV ratings in years, Addison Russell, a 22-year-old shortstop, hit a three-run home run to win over the Cincinnati Reds. The Cubs started the 2016 season with a 6-1 record.

I jumped out of bed and ran into Walker's room declaring, "The Cubs won!" He responded with, "Aren't you suppose to fly that flag?"

"Yes! That's right, I am," I said and I ran off with pride and purpose.

Every time they won, I would fly the **W** flag leaving it on the balcony railing until the morning of the next game. I even strung twinkle lights around the railing so the flag was visible at night. It was a ritualistic display of pride.

One of my neighbors yelled up from the parking lot, "What's the flag mean?"

"It means the Chicago Cubs won today," I yelled back.

He gave me the thumbs up sign. I saw him again in August and he said, "The Cubs are winning a lot this year. I've gotten used to seeing your flag."

"This is the year," I responded.

On April 21, Jake Arrieta, kale-juice-drinking, Sports Illustrated cover model, pitched a no-hitter. That same game, Kris Bryant with his blue eyes, hit two home runs. The Cubs destroyed the Cincinnati Reds, 16-0.

On May 8, Bryce Harper and his beautiful hair came to Wrigley Field with his Washington Nationals. The Cubs walked him six times, which was some sort of record. The rules of baseball

My mom and I in front of the brick monument at Walker Stadium named for my dad and Uncle Rube. The town of Lenoir wanted to honor the two brothers after their epic meeting in 1969 at the National League Division Series. It was dedicated in August 1971, but it was after my dad died. (Photo courtesy of family friend of Ann Walker)

allow for a manager to walk a batter. Since Harper is a phenomenal hitter, Maddon decided to do it every time he came to the plate, making Harper a non-issue. It worked. The Cubs won.

That was the first I remember Maddon's wizardry. Joe Maddon implemented all sorts of interesting strategies throughout the season to promote his philosophy of staying in the moment and enjoying the game. He had a laid-back approach to managing, telling the players to go out there and "try not to suck."

T-shirts were printed with the slogan "Try Not To Suck" with a portion of the proceeds going to Cubs charities so I bought one and adopted the "Maddonism" as my motto. I would tell myself, "Today you are going to do the best you can and try not to suck." It made me smile.

Maddon had the players wear onesie pajamas on a flight home from a West Coast road trip. The next day they won a 13-inning game against the Pittsburgh Pirates at Wrigley Field. He brought a petting zoo to batting practice for the players and their families. There are pictures of Anthony Rizzo holding a snow leopard and Maddon walking the field with a pink flamingo. It loosened the players up creating a casual tone in the dugout that spilled over onto the field. This team was fun to watch.

His game lineup was always changing. He took this group of young players and moved them all around the field. It reminded me of when my oldest son played T-ball. The coach would say, "Walker, today you are going to play first base. On Wednesday, you are in center field". In one game Kris Bryant went from left field to third base to first base. They thrived wherever he put them.

Maddon's calm demeanor, sense of humor, charisma and laid back coaching style reminded me of Dad. Just like my dad, Maddon had never played a single game in the majors. Maybe P.K. Wrigley should have given him a shot at managing all those years ago when my dad asked. He might have been just the motivational mentor the players needed to win.

I had spent the spring getting to know each player and immersing myself in the game. As summer approached, I settled into a comfortable relationship with my Chicago Cubs.

I watched the games at night after my day was done. The flags on the Wrigley scoreboard, the announcer's voices, the camera shots of fans in Cubs swag were all comforting. It reminded me of being there. My pilgrimage that had gone so perfectly. I would get lost in the rhythm of the game. I referred to it as the "Zen of baseball." Watching the Cubs became part of my crusade for calm.

Sue Sacharski, my "go-to" girl for all things Cubs, is an Anthony Rizzo fan. When he jumped onto the right field wall balancing on his big toe, reaching into the stands to catch a foul ball, Sue and I decided that one catch earned him a Golden Glove for 2016. It was a thing of beauty. We marveled at his ability to do the splits keeping his foot on first base and reaching out to catch the ball.

I was a Kris Bryant fan. He was named National League Rookie of the Year in 2015. His boyish charm is equally matched with his baseball ability. On June 27th in a game against the Cincinnati Reds, Bryant hit three home runs and two doubles in the same game going 5 for 5.

Sue and I are Bryzzo – Bryant and Rizzo – fans.

A June 28 match up with the Reds would go 15 innings. In Maddon fashion, three relief pitchers would play left field in a tag team fashion. One relief pitcher would pitch to a batter then relocate to third base and another reliever would take the mound. That happened three times. It was deemed the "left field game."

The high jinks worked; the Cubs won.

173

Then it happened. The Cubs went into a bit of a slump. They were swept by the Mets in a four-game series, then lost three in a row to the Reds and Braves. They looked tired.

The Cubs staggered into the All-Star break having lost 9 of 11 games and the cynics and naysayers were wailing. Years of scar tissue had left even the most devoted Cubs fan waiting for the other shoe to drop. The critics had stayed hidden through the first half of the season because, frankly, there was very little to complain about.

Long-time observers began to squawk. Maddon was over-managing. The young players had hit a wall. The pitching wasn't that good after all. These Cubs would be no different than countless Cubs teams that came before. I found myself in full defense mode but deep down I was a bit worried.

The Cubs continued to struggle after the break. They were just 6-5 in their first 11 games and seemed to be tottering on the brink.

Then on July 25, the Cubs acquired closer Aroldis Chapman from the New York Yankees. It was a bold and controversial acquisition as Chapman was the first player to be suspended under Major League Baseball's new Domestic Violence Policy. Chapman allegedly choked his girlfriend and fired eight shots in the garage of his home.

Charges were not filed against him citing "conflicting accounts and insufficient evidence." However, under the new policy, MLB Commissioner Rob Manfred could impose discipline as he saw fit regardless of whether the case went to trial. Chapman was suspended for 30 games and accepted the suspension.

Still, despite those concerns, Epstein saw Chapman as the final piece of the puzzle the Cubs required to win it all. He was a closer with a triple digit fastball. It proved to be just the jolt they needed because on July 27, the Cubs opened a series with the crosstown White Sox that started a streak which would put the National League Central race to bed.

From July 27 through August 12, the Cubs won 14 of 15 games, including an 11-game winning streak that left every other contender in the dust. My **W** flag was getting no break. My concern subsided but I knew if this didn't work out like I hoped, I was going to be devastated. Just like any other love affair.

I confess, I was not a Jon Lester fan at the start. I thought he was a bit of a diva who couldn't field his position. He also brought with him his own catcher, David Ross, who was 39, which is ancient in baseball.

Lester won me over in a game in late July when he came off the bench in the 12th inning to bunt. He really is a terrible hitter which is fine, as most pitchers are not expected to be hitters, but Maddon brought him in to drive home the guy on third and he executed it flawlessly. The Cubs won.

David Ross, also known as Grandpa Rossy because of his age, had spent 15 years in the big leagues playing for the Los Angeles Dodgers, Pittsburgh Pirates, San Diego Padres, Cincinnati Reds, Boston Red Sox and Atlanta Braves before joining the Cubs in 2015 as Jon Lester's personal catcher.

I was unsure about Ross to start, but 2016 turned into his magical season. It included catching Jake Arrieta's no-hitter, and hitting a home run in Game 7 of the World Series, making him the oldest player in MLB history to do so. He was a valuable presence in the dugout for the younger players. They looked up to him. Realizing there was little else for him to accomplish after helping the Cubs to a World Series title, David Ross retired.

Pedro Strop with his hat slightly to the left, was a reliable set-up man for the Cubs all season and my favorite pitcher from the bullpen. He wore his hat like that because it's comfortable for him – not as a sign of rebellion. I admired his individuality in the face of criticism. He was fined by his previous team for doing it, but Maddon was only concerned with his ability to strike out batters. Pedro is also known for pointing to the heavens after a particularly eventful inning. "I thank God for everything," he said. "I always do." I got to see him pitch and point to the heavens when I went to Wrigley.

Catcher Wilson Contreras had already intrigued fans when he was named the Cubs' minor league player of the year in 2015. He was promoted to the big club in June 2016. In his first plate appearance, he hit the first pitch he saw against the Pittsburgh Pirates for a two-run home run. He was just the 30th player in modern major league history to do so. He looked like a kid rounding home. The fans went wild giving him a standing ovation.

There was Ben Zobrist, the veteran utility player for the Tampa Bay Rays, Oakland A's and Kansas City Royals, who signed a four-year deal in 2016 to join his old manager in Chicago. BenZo was a consistent player especially in the outfield. He used his experience from the 2015 World Series appearance with the Royals to steady the Cubs. In the 2016 World Series, he hit .357 with five runs scored and 10 hits, including the go-ahead RBI double in the 10th inning of Game 7.

I loved what BenZo brought to the team, but he won me over when he posted a video on Instagram singing "Let it Go" from *Frozen* with his daughter.

This was the team that entered the postseason. A collection of young stars like Bryant and Rizzo with veterans like Zobrist and Lester. The only thing stopping them was history.

Summer was ending, the nights were cooler and I was feeling more like myself. I entered the postseason with my team, confident, completely enamored and borderline obsessed.

Dear Cubs,

Baseball is where I feel the closest to my dad right now.
    There is an energy, a life, an excitement. Particularly
    with this team.
It gives me something substantial to hold on to. It makes
    me happy.
This team makes me happy.
I was told once by a wise man, "if you want to get to
    know your dad, learn about his passion, baseball"
When I watch these games, I feel connected to my dad
    through you in some existential way.
So me and a lot of other people are out here watching you
    guys
Fly the W!
LA

The Cubs faced the San Francisco Giants in the National League Division Series. The Giants were always a daunting challenge in the postseason, especially recently in even numbered years – having won the World Series in 2010, 2012 and 2014 while missing the playoffs altogether in the odd numbered years. Since this was 2016, Cubs' fans were concerned.

The Cubs got great pitching performances from Jon Lester and Travis Wood to take the first two games in Chicago.

Game 3 in San Francisco pitted Jake Arrieta against Madison Bumgarner, one of the great postseason pitchers in recent years. Madison has five distinct and effective pitches: four-seam fastball, cut fastball, curve, changeup, and slow curve. He also hails from my native Caldwell County. I grew up in Lenoir and he lives just down the road in Granite Falls. It is literally down Highway 321.

When I spoke with his dad Kevin Bumgarner, I asked him if he had taught Madison how to pitch. He replied, "No, I taught him how to hit." Madison just happened to be one of the most successful hitting pitchers.

MadBum, as he is nicknamed, beat the Cubs in Game 3. But any questions about a collapse were answered the next night when the Cubs put away the Giants, 6-5, winning the series three games to one.

Next up, the Los Angeles Dodgers. The National League Championship Series would determine which team would play in the World Series. This is where the Cubs blew it last year against the Mets, so pre-game trepidation felt normal.

After winning the first game, the Cubs lost the next two. The bats went cold. They were shut out 1-0 and again in Game 3, 6-0, leaving Cubs fans with that nauseatingly familiar feeling of being so close and watching it disintegrate before their eyes.

Luckily, Game 4 in Los Angeles became a Cubs hit fest. Outfielder Matt Szczur was not in the lineup but loaned his bat to Anthony Rizzo who got a hit to end his post season slump to start the Cubs rally ending in a 10-2 victory over the Dodgers. Matt Szczur's bat was deemed lucky.

Addison Russell had also been in a hitting slump and borrowed Szczur's leggings, which are spandex shorts players wear under their uniforms. In the following two games, Russell got five hits, including two home runs.

Szczur was quoted in the *Chicago Tribune*, "People broke out of their slumps and it just so happened to be with my stuff. I feel like a lot of things happen for a reason."

That was followed by an 8-4 win in Game 5, setting up the next one to be played at Wrigley with a crowd of 42,386 in attendance. The streets and bars in Wrigleyville were flooded with fans. The pre-game analysts mentioned Steve Bartman and my head almost blew off. I did feel sorry for poor Bartman, but I did not want to hear his name.

The Bartman incident happened 13 years ago in Game 6 of the NLDS. The Cubs were five outs away from the World Series. They had the Florida Marlins right where they wanted them with ace Mark Prior on the mound and a raucous Wrigley Field crowd ready to explode.

With one out in the top of the eighth inning, Marlins' hitter Luis Castillo lifted a fly ball down the left field line that seemed destined for the stands. Cubs' left fielder, Moises Alou, thought he had a shot to catch it and leapt into the stands. A host of fans, including a guy in a Cubs' cap, head phones and turtleneck named Steve Bartman, stuck their hands up attempting to catch the ball. Instead of the ball being caught by anyone, it bounced off Bartman's hands and Alou went nuts, slamming down his gloves and cursing the fan for interfering.

This changed the course of the game.

What happened from there still guts Cubs fans. Castillo reached base, sure-handed Cubs' shortstop Alex Gonzalez committed an error on a certain double play grounder and the Marlins hit and hit and hit – and hit some more. They scored eight runs that inning to win Game 6. Every Cubs fan knew the series was over even though there was one game left to play. Sure enough, despite taking a 5-3 lead in Game 7, the Cubs did dissolve and they lost.

The mere mention of Bartman made me nervous.

For Game 5, the Dodgers put their ace pitcher Clayton Kershaw on the mound against Kyle Hendricks. Announcer Joe Buck's admiration for Kershaw is well documented but he did not mention Bartman, thank goodness. Kyle Hendricks would pitch the most beautiful game of his career and shut down the Dodgers sending the Cubs to the World Series for the first time since 1945. Our opponent: the Cleveland Indians.

The first thought I had was, "They have to win."

Baseball is a game of failure full of superstition. As a spectator and participant, you make peace with defeat. Anything from voodoo to complex routines before and after the games is implemented to increase odds for success. To appease his superstitions, Joe DiMaggio would run from the outfield and touch second base before heading into the dugout.

For Game 1 of the World Series against the tough and likable Cleveland Indians team, I ordered take-out from a local Latin grill, knowing that if the Cubs won, I would be ordering this very same meal for every World Series game.

I put my **W** flag out on the porch, ready to fly it. Sitting down in front of the game, I texted Sue Sachariski. I was nervous.

> Me: I have heartburn
> Sue: I had the chills
> Me: A-Rod picked Cleveland to win. I hate him for that.

Unfortunately, Cubs' pitcher Jon Lester was not on his game and Alex Rodriguez was right. The Cleveland Indians won.

For Game 2, I did not eat at the previously mentioned Latin grill as I deemed it to be bad luck. I ate Indian food, a lot of it. I kept the **W** flag inside instead of putting it on the porch like I had done the night before. Jake Arrieta was pitching and I felt good about him. Sue declared herself bad luck and refused to watch the game. We texted again.

> Me: I support you in your superstition and will alert you when the Cubs take the lead.
> Sue: I'm watching an old John Wayne movie, "The Sands of Iwo Jima."
> Me: The Indians pitcher has 10 stitches in his pinky,

Cubs 1-0, Joe Buck is killing me.
Sue: John Wayne just got killed by a sniper.
Me: Is that the end? Keep watching movies the
Cubs 2-0

The Cubs won. They were headed home. Theo Epstein, president of baseball operations, is quoted as saying, "Families are connecting with one another, generations.... It's so many things on so many levels."

I looked at my dad's picture in his baseball uniform. I thought about the generations of Chicago Cubs fans steeped in the tradition of optimism for the lovable losers. Family memories, fathers and daughters, friendships, nourished by the rebirth of hope each spring and the acceptance of defeat each fall. The continuity, year after year, bound us together in some sick yet fantastical folklore. It was about more than just baseball. Theo was right.

The win in Game 2 was followed by more good news. Kyle Schwarber, the guy hurt only a week into the season, was back in the lineup. I considered that a positive omen.

For Game 3, Cubs' great Billy Williams was throwing out the ceremonial first pitch. Actor and die-hard Cubs' fan Bill Murray would sing "Take Me Out to the Ballgame" during the 7th inning stretch. I ordered Indian food. It seemed perfect.

Until the offense shut down and Cleveland posted wins of 1-0 and 7-2 in Games 3 and 4 to take a daunting three games to one lead. No team had ever come back from a two-game deficit. I called my mom after the third loss.

"I guess they aren't going to do it again this year. At least they made it this far," she declared trying to cushion the blow.

"Don't say it! I won't be happy with just getting here," I said sounding more certain than I probably felt. "They are going to win tonight. They have to," I declared.

"We'll see. I'm pulling for them," she responded.

I didn't call her again until the Series was over. I refused to consider that the Cleveland Indians could win the World Series at Wrigley Field. My love affair could not end like this. I took the color 8x10 glossy of my dad, the one that showed off his eyes, and propped it up on my bedside table. I was going to symbolically watch Game 5 with him.

I knew one thing for sure. I wasn't going to eat Chicken Tikka Masala.

Lester pitched, making me insanely nervous, but he pitched well. Kris Bryant started a rally with a home run. Eddie Vedder of Pearl Jam sang during the 7th inning stretch, dedicating it to former Cubs broadcaster Harry Caray. Chapman got himself in and out of a jam, but didn't allow the Indians to score.

The Cubs won, 3-2, forcing a Game 6 in Cleveland, and staying alive for at least one more game

If they were to win their first World Series in 108 years, it would have to be done in Cleveland, a franchise which hadn't won a World Series of its own since 1948. In most seasons, the Indians would be a team I could have rooted for as they were a classic underdog. But not this year.

The next night was Halloween and a travel day for the Cubs. I dressed up like a butterfly and took my kids trick-or-treating in my new neighborhood. I needed a break from baseball. It was good to be a butterfly for a few hours.

November 1 at 8 p.m., I was watching Game 6 and cheering for the Cubs. There was an uneasy nervousness in my stomach. This could be the last night I watched this particular team, my Cubs. These were the guys who had carried me through a challenging year. Going into Game 6, I had a mix of excitement, apprehension, terror, and hope. This struck me as the four horsemen of the relationship apocalypse.

Dear Lord, let my love affair continue. I put the picture of my dad on my bedside table as I had done for Game 5.

> Sue: Are you gonna watch this with me sister?
> Me: Hell yessssss
> Sue: I've got Pat and Ron on the radio
> Me: Jakes beard is outta control
> Sue: Really! Like 1800s outta control
> Me: I'm going to take a shower. Every time I do that the Cubs do something great and I miss it
> Sue: Take as long as you like
> Me: I came back to see the bases loaded
> Sue: ADDY!

The Cubs came out strong in the first inning with a 3-0 lead. It was just the start I was hoping for. Arrieta's pitching was on point. Then baby-faced Addison Russell hit a grand slam home run increasing the Cubs lead to 7-0.

The Cubs won Game 6, 9-3. I did cartwheels down the hallway like a kid. When I woke up on November 2nd, the day of Game 7, I broke out in hives. I wrote to Sue and told her I had hives on my chest and neck. She said it was Cubitis: a disease for which there is no cure.

I would like to tell you that my anxiety decreased because I used all my meditation tools and power of positive thinking to calm me into a state of serenity. But I can't. My anxiety increased exponentially as the hours ticked by, leading up to the first pitch. My kids were with me, thank goodness. I explained to them the two scenarios that could potentially go down.

The first scenario: we were going to celebrate by cartwheeling down the hallway and running through the court yard carrying the **W** flag. The second? They would have to pick me up off the kitchen floor where I would be lying face down in a pool of my own tears.

I was itchy, twitchy, sweaty and exhausted. Little did I know the Cubs would take me from full blown Cubitis to the brink of a nervous breakdown in the next four hours. I got this message from Sue:

> Sue: Yesterday was a Holy Day of Obligation. I took
> mom to mass. We both admitted to praying for the
> Cubs. Today is All Souls Day. Think of our dads
> and the millions of Cubs fans on our side tonight

Her message shifted my thoughts and, for a split second, I allowed myself to feel the complete joy of being right here getting ready to watch my team play in Game 7 of the World Series. I ordered Thai food.

Game 7 will go down in history as one of the best baseball games ever played. That's not just my opinion. I've heard the truest of baseball fans say it.

> Sue: 4th inning feels like the 14th
> Me: Lester is warming up?
> Sue: Lester will get your hives going again
> Me: I hate Lester right now but if he gets Kipnis out
> I will love him again
> Sue: haha! Love/hate/love
> Me: It's my pattern. I'm in therapy for it
> Sue: I keep visualizing all the spirits filling the field,
> helping this team
> Me: That helps me relax

Overhearing a conversation in the dugout between

Anthony Rizzo and David Ross helped me, too. FOX Sports had placed mics strategically in dugouts during the games allowing the TV audience to listen in on some conversations between players or coaches.

> Rizzo: I can't control myself right now. I'm trying my best.
> Ross: It's understandably so, buddy.
> Rizzo: I'm emotional.
> Ross: I hear ya.
> Rizzo: I'm an emotional wreck.
> Ross: Well, it's only going to get worse. Just continue to breathe. That's all you can do, buddy. It's only gonna get worse.
> Rizzo: I'm in a glass case of emotion right now.
> Ross: Wait until the 9th with this three-run lead

David Ross's words must have helped because Rizzo got a hit his next at bat.

The Cubs had a 6-3 comfortable lead going into the eighth inning, six outs away. A double and a two-run home run by the Indians tied the game in the eight. Neither team was able to score in the ninth and the game went into extra innings. At this point both my kids went to bed. It was a school night after all, and I was a wreck.

Then the rain delay happened. Perfectly timed as if it was the cumulative tears cascading from heaven from all the scar tissue. I had 17 minutes to pace around. Then the thought came in my mind: I just need this to be over. I can't take it anymore!

The suspense was killing me. I was at the end of my tether drained from dangling in this heightened state of emotion for two weeks.

I glanced in my closet. I was not going back there to hide. I walked onto my balcony instead. I didn't dare touch or even look at my **W** flag. I stood in the night air, breathing it in and out. Looking up at the sky, thinking of my dad, I said out loud, "Are you watching this?"

If he was watching the Cubs and me, he was proud of us both.

Returning to my bedroom, I looked at the picture of my dad propped up against my bedside lamp and sat down on the edge of my bed, both feet on the ground, arms wrapped in front of me. My stomach was growling, my heart was racing, and my palms were sweaty. The Cubs scored 2 runs in the 10th. All they had to do now was get 3 outs.

The Indians scored in the 10th. With 2 outs and a runner on first, the batter hit a soft ground ball to Kris Bryant at third base. As Bryant threw the ball to Anthony Rizzo for the last out, I put my hand over my mouth in disbelief saying out loud, "Dear God, they did it." They were two games down and won the World Series.

> Sue: sobbing for JOY
> Me: this is real, right? Not a dream
> Sue: it's true

Cubs flooded the infield, colliding into each other in pure elation. I was frozen there at the end of my bed, transfixed watching the celebration. I had been present for it all – from opening day to Game 7.

My heart was full. This win represented struggle, perseverance, family, tradition, passion, and for me a final chapter to the book I would eventually write. The last leg of my journey brought me full circle back to the place I started. Baseball.

The sun rose on my **W** flag.

"I told you they would do it!" I gloated to my mom.

"You were right. They pulled it off," she replied.

"Did you watch the whole thing?" I asked, wondering if she had dozed off at some point.

"I did. I was on pins and needles, pacing back and forth," she said with a laugh.

I almost asked her what she thought dad might say, but I didn't. I left it alone. I wasn't sad, I was grateful. I no longer needed someone to tell me how my dad might feel or what he might say. I knew. He would smile and say "finally" about us both – me and the Cubs.

My love affair had a storybook ending.

Dear Dad,

I put my life on hold from October 25 – November 2, to savor every moment of these games. I hate that it's over, but I love the way it ended.

I'm gonna miss this. I'll find another way to connect with you.

Maybe you will come visit me in my dreams again.

You, with the help of the Chicago Cubs, have delivered me from melancholy.

I love you

LA

PS. Do you see how awesome my kids are?

EXTRA INNINGS
Make a Legacy List

*H*ere's the thing. I have stepped into myself. I no longer feel uncomfortable in the skin I was given. I was looking for something outside of me and this journey was my roadmap to myself.

From a bed in Wesley Memorial Hospital in Chicago, one of my father's last requests was that I be well educated. I can assume that he wanted me to be smart, independent and capable of taking care of myself.

The main thing I discovered is that I stepped into a strength that grounded me and that I didn't have before. I was walking through the pain and coming through the other side. I realized there's a part of my dad I carry with me all the time now.

It's funny, as much as I thought I needed to hear my dad's voice to somehow connect me to him, hearing that voice almost became a non-issue. The voice was the spark, but now I have so much more. I thought hearing his voice was what I was going for, but it was the journey I was looking for. The journey turned out to be so much more important. It allowed me to access the grief.

I was looking for something outside of me but I realized he was inside of me all along. Maybe it took me talking to so many people and hearing so much about my father and who he was and what he meant to so many people for me to understand that. That realization has brought me a more secure feeling inside of me than a voice ever did.

I wanted more advice from my father. We all have life lessons we can share with loved ones and friends. I have the luxury of time with my boys and seriously love every minute we are together. I decided to put together a list for them. I call it a "Legacy List."

I encourage you to compile a "legacy list" of your own. It is an exercise in self-discovery as well as a wonderful way to leave your words for your loved ones.

Trust me, it will bring someone comfort one day.

> *To My Beautiful Boys:*
>
> *If I die tomorrow this is what I want you to know. I'm making a list for you so there is no doubt in your mind how I feel about things. We have spent many hours together, so you know me. But time has a way of fading memories. You might one day wonder how I might feel about certain life situations. Hopefully I will still be around to ask. But in case I'm not, let me start by saying a few things before I get to my legacy list.*
>
> *I'm a liberal democrat, but if you run for public office as a republican, I will still love you. Any girl that you love, I will love, too. Until she hurts you and then I'm done. Don't drive drunk. Call me instead. I will come and get you without any questions. When you mess up, I will help you without judgment. If your dream is to join the circus, I will support your decision because I am not a dream killer.*
>
> ### *My Legacy List*
>
> 1. *Be on time. Return phone calls. If you say you're going to do something, do it.*

2. *Your thoughts are powerful. Keep them positive.*

3. *Money will come and money will go. Don't let it define you or anyone else.*

4. *Get out of the problem and into the solution.*

5. *Listen to the voice deep inside you, always.*

6. *People generally don't do things to you, they do things for themselves. Try not to take it personally and move on.*

7. *Laugh loud and often.*

8. *Stay clear of anyone who cites the writings of Ayn Rand as being influential to their life, especially the novel Atlas Shrugged. They are selfish.*

9. *Don't be afraid to try new things.*

10. *If you need advice about girls, ask a girl. Boys don't understand girl world.*

11. *Random acts of kindness will heal you. When you are troubled or worried do something for another person, just because you can.*

12. *If you meet someone who has no friends from the past, that's a red flag. Chances are they live life intensely and burn bridges. They will probably be charismatic but there is a reason nobody from the past is around.*

13. *If you get the chance—travel. See the world. It will give you perspective.*

14. *Physical and emotional pain have a purpose. It will show you what you need to change about yourself, your life, or a particular situation. Pay attention to it.*

15. *Crying is a normal reaction to sadness. If you don't cry out all the tears they stay inside you and make you sick and angry.*

16. *Make mistakes and ask questions. That is how you learn.*

17. *You will be afraid and you will get lonely. Know deep*

in your heart that you came into this world loved and with great purpose. You will be okay.

18. *Practice gratitude every day. This is the key to consistent happiness. I have literally tried everything else.*
19. *Education is important. Always be eager to learn from people, books, classes, situations and mistakes.*
20. *Multi-tasking is overrated. Focus on one thing at a time.*
21. *Eat healthy food, drink lots of water, and wear sunscreen.*
22. *If something doesn't feel right, don't do it.*
23. *You have my approval; waste no more time on that. I am your biggest fan.*
24. *I loved every minute with you. I remember it all. You were all I ever wanted.*

Being your guide through life has been a privilege and a great pleasure, even the yucky stuff.

I love you deeply,
Mom

This has been a deeply personal glimpse into my life. I have labored over every word. My hope is that it might help someone in their struggle with grief. I hope this has proven that it is never too late to confront the loss, to start over, to redesign your life.

Remember when I referred to myself as a little lost star with no gravity? It turns out, stars have their own gravity. I had it all along. This was a journey to unlock what was already inside me, what is inside all of us.

A few other lessons I learned along the way are:

A legacy can be created by small acts of kindness.

Surrender is more powerful than struggle.

There is purpose in the pain.

Once you let the problem go, the solution can enter.

I was encumbered by grief. This journey did emancipate me. I found my dad and I found myself. Writing this book brought me full circle and further healed me. I am equal parts afraid that nobody will read it, and that somebody will read it.

In the beginning, I wanted to learn more about the father I never knew. Thanks to the generosity and consideration of many people, I now know Verlon Walker. In the end, I needed to take a journey inside myself. Thanks to the support of many, I had the courage to do that.

I learned that he was a good man who made good decisions. He was kind. He had a dry, self-deprecating sense of humor that endeared him to many – from the people he grew up with in Lenoir, to the woman he married, to the coaches he worked alongside, to the players he competed with and against. It didn't matter if they were rookies or Hall of Famers, my dad treated each one decently. He had a positive spirit that made everyone feel good in his presence.

I am thankful he proved to be an extraordinary man. He would have been an incredible father and grandfather.

He has been with me all along. I see it now and it's evident in pieces of my personality. I feel him with me too. So, this is where it ends with love and respect for my father, myself and my journey.

All of it has been a baseball love story.

Editor's Note
by Chuck Carlson

*L*eigh Ann Walker includes this email from former Major Leaguer Terry Kennedy in her book. It is powerful and heartbreaking and says everything you need to know about Verlon Walker, his daughter's journey of discovery and her book that delves deep into the places we all have but few can acknowledge.

> My dad (Bob Kennedy) was manager when your father was coach with the Cubs. I remember your father well even though I was only 8 years old. You don't forget someone that nice. My father was a good judge of character and he loved your dad.
>
> I remember when I would go on the field in my own little flannel Cubs uniform and play catch with whoever was out there. I threw a few with your dad. Now, my father is gone too. It doesn't matter what age you are there is always loss (I was 49 when he passed). I have followed your quest and wish you well…..I will pray for you in your search and as one baseball kid to another, I understand. Perhaps, as you have mentioned, it's not the prize but the journey that will fulfill your dream.

Verlon Walker died of leukemia in March 1971, at the height of spring training. He had been promoted to pitching coach for the Chicago Cubs that season but he never got the chance to coach. He was just 42 when he died and he left behind his wife Ann and the light of his life, Leigh Ann, who was just 3.

I didn't know Verlon Walker and, in truth, had never even heard of him until I began working with Leigh Ann on this book that, as she told me on numerous occasion, she had to write. I didn't really understand that when we started; I understand it only too well now.

And as much as this was Leigh Ann's long-time journey to find out all she could about her father, I ended up going on that same trip. I learned how rare it is for people to go through life leaving memories of good will and affection and admiration in their wake as they go. And I learned that Verlon Walker seemed to do that everywhere he went and with everyone he met. That's a rare gift.

So when I read the passage from Terry Kennedy, I began to understand a little about who Verlon was, what he meant to so many people and why his daughter, after so many years of running away from his memory, needed to run head-long into it.

This was not an easy project to start or complete. And, frankly, it was no bargain in the middle either. Writers, by their very nature, are never happy with anything we do. A misplaced phrase, a poor choice of words, taking three hours to make sure one paragraph is exactly right. And even then, there's something wrong. Writers are annoying, petulant, exasperating types.

And first-time writers? Oh my, they're even worse to the point where I talked Leigh Ann off more than a few metaphorical cliffs as she peered, horrified, into the gaping chasm of self-doubt.

She knew she had a great story to tell. A story of loss and grief and unhappiness and renewal and redemption and, yes, enlightenment. But, as with every writer, she wasn't sure if anyone would want to read what she had to say.

I wasn't sure at first either. But Leigh Ann opened herself up emotionally in ways I'm not sure as a professional writer I would want to do, or could do. And I admire her for that.

She left the ubiquitous "comfort zone" everyone says that they want to break out from but rarely do, and headed to places she'd never been before. It was an arduous trip but she did it because she knew that was the only way to tell her story the way it needed to be told.

This is not a sports book in the classic sense. It is a book about a family – Verlon and Ann Walker, and Uncle Rube and Leigh Ann – and how loss, no matter how long ago it was, can continue to reverberate through the years.

It is a book about the determination to overcome the unknown and finding the strength to find the answers to the questions you weren't sure you could ask.

It is a book about dealing with the ache and longing of grief and realizing that it never really goes away but, if you're lucky, it can find a place inside you where it doesn't hurt quite so much.

But mostly, it is a book about the impact one man, Verlon Walker, had on so many people. Terry Kennedy said it before, "You don't forget a man that nice."

And those are the memories that endure.

Acknowledgements

I did not take this journey alone. I assembled an amazing team along the way. Each person played a unique role in my journey. With a grateful heart, I thank you.

Ann Walker - We both lost him. You bravely took this time-travel journey with me. You have an unshakable faith that gives you strength in all situations. I am a good mother because you were. Thank you for nurturing my carefree spirit and for loving my children with your big BaBa heart.

Walker and Christopher - Thank you for not caring one bit about this. Being your mom is the highlight of my life. You are my heart.

Pat Hughes - Thank you for returning my email, taking an interest in me, connecting me to the right people and giving me a media pass to see you at Wrigley.

Leigh Ann Stacy Alexander - Your encouragement propelled me forward. Without you, I'm quite sure, I would have given up. I walk through the world with swagger because you locked arms with me in second grade and haven't let go. I attribute my extensive musical library to your guidance. Laughing with you healed my heart. I love you.

Dennis Young - Thank you for the baseball glove, the message that accompanied it and for picking blackberries for me.

George Castle - You were the manager; I was the rookie. Your instruction brought me to the big show. You made me work hard and dream big. "You can do this Carolina Girl," you said. You believed, so I did too.

Keith Olbermann – Thank you for the beautiful way you shared my story.

Barbie, Debbie and Janet - (Al "Rube" Walker's daughters) You sent me love just when I needed it. Reconnecting with all of you has been a blessing.

Sue Sacharski - You are my soul sister, my Chicago driver, my Cubs confidante. The World Series was made more enjoyable because I shared it with you. I am honored to have you in my life. #flytheW

Mary Deese - You were the first woman I encountered on my quest. An oasis of femininity in the middle of all those men. The way you spoke to me opened my heart. You checked on me, you fed me, you made me laugh. Thank you for the carefully organized mailed packages of pictures and memorabilia.

Greg Carlton -. You vividly shared your memories with me which gave me a unique glimpse of my dad. Those other stories you told me, I will keep to myself. As you said, "What happens in the dugout, stays in the dugout"

Chuck Carlson - My encourager. I appreciate your soft guidance as we plowed through this project which at times felt like we were digging a pit with a toothpick.

Meredith Jackson - I unraveled and you loved me back together. You didn't wait for me to ask for help, you just

Acknowledgements

helped. That fire walk was easier because I was wrapped in your love.

John Wilson - You have been a consistent source of kindness and love. You always remember my birthday and make me feel special.

Preston Stone - Thank you for the **W** flag, encouraging words, and unwavering belief in me. You helped me access my inner Wonder Woman.

Marian Nisbet - When I grow up, I want to be as fabulous as you. Thank you for assisting in my healing journey.

Sean Dunbar - You inspired me to continue at points when I wanted to give up. Thank you for making me laugh, practicing yoga beside me, drinking purple rain with me, bringing me rocks from Costa Rica, and much much more.

Anne Geary - You helped me inject my soul into this book.

Bessie Tate - Thank you for loving me just as I am and for being my spiritual advisor.

Tammy Bell - You taught me how to save myself.

Teresa Sosinski - I appreciate your tireless efforts correcting my mistakes. I hope to meet you someday.

Bob Snodgrass - Thank you for taking a chance on me and calmly handling my panic attacks.

About the Authors

Ted Hoeffer

This is **Leigh Ann Walker's** first writing project but it's one that has been years in the making. She has a BA degree from Lees-McRae College in North Carolina and her story has been featured on MLB.com, the Charlotte Observer, and ESPN. She lives in Charlotte, North Carolina with her two sons, Walker and Christopher.

Chuck Carlson has been a professional writer for more than 35 years, most of it as a sports writer/columnist and editor at various newspapers around the country. He has written 14 books ranging on topics from the Green Bay Packers to the Milwaukee Brewers to golf. He is now director of media relations at Albion College in Michigan and lives in Marshall, Michigan with his family.

Index

Find out more about Leigh Ann Walker's search for her father's voice at www.baseballlovestory.com

Visit www.ascendbooks.com for more great titles on your favorite teams and athletes.